Programming for Linguists

Programming for Linguists: Java™ Technology for Language Researchers

Michael Hammond

Blackwell
Publishers

© Michael Hammond 2002

Editorial Offices:
108 Cowley Road, Oxford OX4 1JF, UK
  Tel: +44 (0)1865 791100
350 Main Street, Malden, MA 02148-5018, USA
  Tel: +1 781 388 8250

First published 2002 by Blackwell Publishers Ltd, a Blackwell Publishing company

Library of Congress Cataloging-in-Publication Data has been applied for.

ISBN 0-631-23041-6 (hardback); ISBN 0-631-23042-4 (paperback)

A catalogue record for this title is available from the British Library.

Set in 10.5 on 13 pt Sabon
by Graphicraft Limited, Hong Kong
Printed and bound in Great Britain
by T.J. International, Padstow, Cornwall

For further information on
Blackwell Publishers, visit our website:
www.blackwellpublishers.co.uk

Contents

Preface

This book addresses the fact that computational literacy is essential for the modern linguist or related language professional; for example, speech pathologists, psycholinguists, literary theorists, and so on. Simple programming expertise is an essential part of many forms of data collection and analysis in these fields. Unfortunately, people interested in language often have little or no math background and are sometimes put off by typical programming courses.

This book undertakes to introduce a completely naive person to the rudiments of Java™ programming. Through a series of simple examples and exercises, the reader is gradually introduced to the essentials of good programming. The examples are carefully constructed so as to make the introduction of new concepts as simple as possible, while at the same time using sample programs that make sense to someone who works with language as data. Many of these programs can be used immediately with minimal or no modification.

How is this Book Different?

A number of Java textbooks and manuals are available. How is this book different from the rest?

First, the most important respect in which this book is different is that it focuses on language. The book is intended for readers interested in using Java programming to help them understand language.

Second, unlike many books, every example given is a full program and can stand alone. Thus, for the reader starting from scratch, there is minimal mystery in applying material from any example.

Third, the book is written for a naive reader who may know *nothing* about programming. No prior programming experience is assumed *whatsoever*.

Finally, the book focuses on very usable code in Java 1.1. Many Java programming books succumb to the temptation of treating the absolute most recent version of the Java programming language, but the most recent version is far from the most useful. While I treat Java 1.2 and 1.3 – both also referred to as Java 2 – in appendix A, the body of the book deals with the version of the Java technology that runs on virtually every platform and that can run in web browsers.

What this Book Isn't

This is not a book on computational linguistics. We spend no time modeling linguistic theory or discussing theory of any sort. Readers interested in language but who have no interest in modern linguistic theory should have no fear that knowledge of that field might be required or that we will be preoccupied with the minutiae of linguistic theory.[1]

This book is not a compendium on Java programming. There are many details that are left aside. The goal is to expose the naive reader with an interest in language to the most usable aspects of Java technology, those most relevant for writing programs that deal with language.[2]

Website

The text is accompanied by exercises at the end of each chapter and all the code is available from the companion websites at http://www.blackwell.com and http://www.u.arizona.edu/~hammond.

Versions

Java technology has changed over the years since it was introduced. There are four principal versions: 1.0, 1.1, 1.2, and 1.3. In this book, I stick to version 1.1 as much as possible. This is for two reasons. First, even though Java 1.2 has been out for several years, most web browsers are still not capable of running applets written with 1.2. In addition, while 1.2, and now 1.3, are both available for Windows and Solaris, the most recent version has only become available for Macintosh with Mac OS 10. In the spirit of true platform independence therefore, this book focuses on Java 1.1. Occasionally, the book departs from 1.1, but those points are always noted in the text or in a footnote. Moreover, in appendix A, I treat the main features that distinguish these different versions of Java programming.

Notes

[1] Though how anybody could be left cold by all those little details is a mystery to the linguist–author!

[2] For example, we spend no time on threading and minimal time with graphics.

Michael Hammond
September 2001

Acknowledgments

I would like to thank Sonya Bird, Sheila Dooley-Colberg, Andrea Heiberg, Will Lewis, Tania Zamuner, and several anonymous reviewers for useful comments; and Sarah Coleman, Tami Kaplan, and Beth Remmes at Blackwell for helping get this to print. Any errors are mine alone.

I would also like to thank my wife Diane and my constant programming partner Puck – and especially my son Joe, for introducing me to Java programming in the first place. This book is dedicated to our friend Joyce Drake, who was a model of strength to us in her battle against cancer.

Chapter 1

Why Programming and Why Java™ Programming?

This chapter provides two central premises for the rest of the book. First, why would a linguist, psycholinguist, literary theorist, and so on want to know anything about programming? Second, why would Java programming be a good choice?

1.1 Why Programming?

Working with language data is nearly impossible these days without a computer. Data are massaged, analyzed, sorted, and distributed on computers. There are various software packages available for language researchers, but to truly take control of this domain, some amount of programming expertise is essential. Consider the following simple examples.

Imagine you are a syntactician interested in the use of present-tense verbs. You have an electronic corpus and want to find all the cases of verbs in the present tense. How do you do it?

You're a literary stylist and want to investigate the distribution of words with iambic stress in Milton's poetry.

Imagine you are a phonologist. You're interested in consonant clusters. You have an electronic dictionary and want to find the largest word-final consonant cluster. Do you go through it by hand?

Finally, you're a psycholinguist and you want to perform an experiment to investigate how people syllabify nonsense words.

All of these are fairly typical research tasks. If you don't know how to program yourself, you have only limited options. One possibility is to do the job by hand. For example, the syntactician could simply print out the corpus and go through it line by line. If the corpus is small enough, this might not be so onerous, but if the corpus is large, or if one really wants to be sure of one's results, then this method is fraught with peril (and really boring). Another solution is to hire somebody else to do the job, but the same considerations apply. Yet a third possibility is to make use of some existing software package.

This last option is occasionally workable, but can fall short in several ways. First, an existing package is restricted by its design. That is, your needs may not match what the software was designed to do, rendering your task impossible or very difficult. Moreover, the software may not be intuitive, and may require learning some arcane set of commands or some difficult control language. Finally, while software may exist to do what you want, it may be unavailable on the platform you work on (Windows, Mac, or Unix), or it may be too costly.

1.2   *Why Java Technology?*

The **Java** programming language may provide an answer. First, it is a complete programming language, with all the bells and whistles. It can do all the file manipulation and text searching one might want, while at the same time, it has all the graphical capabilities of a language like C.

Moreover, it's *free*. There are free Java implementations for every type of computer. In addition, code written and compiled on one type of machine will run on any other type. In other words, you can write your code at home on your Mac, and run it at work on your Windows machine, or send it to a colleague to run under Unix. This also suggests that Java programs you write should continue to be usable for many years, since the language is so widely used.

Finally, one of the most compelling features of Java programs is the fact that they can be run over the web in your web browser. What this means is that you can write a program, put it on the web, and allow others to run your program on their own machines simply by going to your web page.

The only downside is that since the Java language can do so much, it can be quite complex. There are lots and lots of features that enable Java programs to do pretty much anything you want. For the novice programmer, this can be intimidating.

We won't let this deter us though. My strategy will be to pick and choose. I'll introduce those bits of Java technology that are necessary to do the kinds of things people who work with language typically want to do. The rest – all the bells and whistles that we don't need on our train – we'll leave for later. I'll let you know where they are and how to find out more, but we won't digress to deal with them here.

1.3   Download and Install the Java Development Kit

Before going on to actually writing Java programs, your computer must be properly configured so that the software for developing programs is available. You must make sure that the **Java Development Kit** (JDK) is installed on your computer. If it is, the command java -version, when typed at the system prompt, will print out appropriate version information. (For a Mac, where there is no system prompt, you must do a search for the program javac, using the Find File command in the Finder.)

If you don't find java or javac on your system, the JDK can be downloaded for free over the web. The appropriate URL is http://www.javasoft.com. Versions of the JDK for Windows and Solaris can be downloaded directly from that site. For other computer types, there are links there to the appropriate site.

It's really very easy to install the JDK, but if you find it daunting at the beginning, you might find it easier to work on a computer that already has the JDK installed. Most mainframe computers have it already installed. If you have access to one – through work or school – you might try running the early programs in the book there.

Let's briefly go over how to install the JDK under Windows. The first step is to download the JDK installer over the web. This is a huge file and you should arrange carefully how to do this. If you have a dedicated very fast connection, there's no problem, but if you want to install the JDK at home over the phone, you need to plan carefully. Depending on the speed of your modem, the download could take *hours*.

If you plan to download the file by phone, you might want to curl up with a book while doing so. Alternatively, it is possible, for a fee, to obtain the JDK on CD-ROM. Finally, if you have ethernet access at work, download the file there, and bring it home on a zip disk.

The JDK installer is typically downloaded in compressed form. For Windows, zip compression is the easiest one to deal with. (For example, in Windows 98, the compressed zip file can be uncompressed automatically.)

Once uncompressed, the second step is to run the install program. This will create a directory called something like j2dk1.x, where x is the version number.

The third step is to add the java and javac programs to your path. This is done by editing your autoexec.bat file. Note that this is something you have to be very careful with. Make sure to make a backup copy of your autoexec.bat file *before* editing it, and make sure to consult your documentation if you've never done this before. First, select the MS-DOS prompt from the Programs menu. Second, type cd \ to switch to the root directory. Type copy autoexec.bat autoexec.bak to make a copy of your autoexec.bat file. Third, type edit autoexec.bat to edit the file. Use the arrow keys to move to the first empty line at the end of the file. Add the following line set path=%PATH%;\j2dk1.x\bin, where x is the appropriate version number in the directory installed. Finally, select quit from the file menu to quit the edit program, making sure to save your changes when prompted. The change will take place when Windows is next started.

Analogous steps are needed to install the JDK under Unix. For Macs, there are different compression options, and the relevant directory is MRJ SDK x, where x is the appropriate version number. There is no Mac path to alter.

1.4   How to Read this Book

Learning to program isn't really hard, but you do need to do it the right way. The key is to start programming right away. As you read this book, you should make sure to try out the programs as we go through them. In fact, it would be ideal to read the book *at the computer*. Also, don't forget to try the exercises! You'll note that answers are not given at the end of the book. This is for two reasons. First, having answers is a big temptation. More importantly, however, most of the exercises involve revising or writing programs. There are often many ways to achieve the same goal and I would rather you find *some* way to answer an exercise question than feel you have to find *my* way of answering one of them.

Start by running the programs exactly as given, either by downloading them from the website or – even better – by typing them in yourself. (Typing them in yourself will make the task familiar and draw your attention to aspects of the code you might miss otherwise.)

When you start to feel more comfortable, try varying the code a bit. The programs up through chapter 3 are perfectly safe and variations can't harm your computer. After that point, certain operations should be handled with care, but I'll warn you about those as we go through.

The key, though, is to have fun!

Chapter 2
Getting Started

This chapter explains how the Java programming language works and introduces the edit–compile–run cycle for readers with no background in programming. I begin with how to edit a file using any number of editors and go on to explain how to compile and run the programs we write. The chapter concludes with a description of how the Java language is different from other programming environments; for example, **bytecode** and the **Java Virtual Machine**.

2.1   Edit, Compile, Run

Just in case you've never written a computer program in your life, let's go over the basic idea. A programming language allows you to issue instructions to your computer. In effect, it is a lingua franca, a mediating language. You translate your ideas into it and the computer translates it into something it can understand: **machine code**.

The process of writing up your program in the programming language is the **edit** phase. Once you've written out your program in the Java language, you then convert it to machine code using the javac command. This is referred to as the **compile** phase. Finally, you **run** your program using the java command. Let's go through each of these in turn.

2.1.1   Edit

You need to create your program using some sort of text editor. In principle, you can use any editor, but it's easiest to use a very simple one. There are a number of possibilities and I list some of them below. The key component is that the file you create needs to be saved as a **text** file with the extension ".java". This can certainly be done with a normal text editor, but is often easier to do with one of these:

Windows   Edit, notepad, Vim, and so on.
Mac   SimpleText, Alpha, BBEdit, and so on.
Unix   Emacs, Vi(m), Pico, and so on.

Let's go through how to create a program using the **DOS** command edit under Windows. First, open the MS-DOS prompt on the program menu of Windows. Switch to an appropriate directory using the cd command. For example, if you plan to put all your Java programs in a directory that you've created called myjava, you would switch to that directory using the command cd \myjava.[1]

Once you're in the appropriate directory, it's time to edit a Java program file. To create a Java program file called HelloWorld.java, type the following in the DOS window: edit HelloWorld.java. This will bring up a simple text editor into which we will type our code. Type the following into the window *exactly*:

```
public class HelloWorld {
    public static void main(String argv[]) {
        System.out.println("Hello World!");
    }
}
```

Tabbing is optional, but helps to show the organization of the program.

When the above code is typed into the edit window, it should look like the following:

To save your code, select save from the File menu. Then choose quit from the same menu to exit back to the DOS window.

Let's go through the code that you typed in very briefly. I'll treat it in more depth later on, but let's just get a sense of what you just did. First, programs have two basic organizational units: **statements** and **groups**. Statements are instructions for the computer to carry out. They are always terminated by a semicolon and are executed in sequence from top to bottom. Groups indicate the organization of statements into larger units and are always marked with curly braces.

Our program contains two nested groups. First, there is a group indicating that this is a program called HelloWorld. Whenever you write a file, the outermost layer of the code will indicate what the name of the program is and must match the name of the file (this is an *extremely* common source of errors, so be careful . . .):

```
public class HelloWorld {
    . . .
}
```

The next layer of grouping, labeled with the keyword main, indicates what the computer should do first when the program is invoked:

```
public static void main(String argv[]) {
    . . .
}
```

Finally, there is the substantive part of the program. In this case, there is only one **command**, or **statement**:

```
System.out.println("Hello World!");
```

This statement has two parts: the **function** System.out.println(), which tells the Java program to print something, and "Hello World!", the **argument** to the function, in this case what it should print. There are many more details and nuances to even this little snippet of code, but I'll defer these to later.

2.1.2   Compile

The next step is to translate your program into something that your computer will understand. You do this with the javac command. You'll type this in at the DOS prompt. For the program we wrote above, simply type the following: javac HelloWorld.java.

The computer should whir away for a few seconds and then stop. If everything has gone as it should, it will simply provide you with another DOS prompt. In the background, it will have created a new file: HelloWorld.class. You can check that this is so with the DOS command dir.

More likely, something went wrong and javac spit out some mysterious error message. Don't despair! This is very very typical. If something has gone wrong, there are really only three possibilities. One is that you did not actually create the HelloWorld.java file or did not save it in the right form. To check this under Windows, type the following: type HelloWorld.java. The file should scroll by in a legible form.

If that worked, and javac HelloWorld.java still doesn't work, then you must have made some sort of error in typing in the original program. Open the file again with your text editor and confirm that it is exactly as above.

A third possibility under Windows or Unix is that javac is not in your path. Follow the instructions appropriate to your operating system to correct this. For Windows, this typically involves editing the autoexec.bat file. For Unix, this typically involves making changes to your .login file or your .cshrc file (or its equivalent).

2.1.3   Run

It's now time to run your program. To do so, type java HelloWorld at the DOS prompt. Notice that the command is now java, not javac. Notice too that no file extension is given for HelloWorld when you use the java command. If everything has been done properly, the phrase "Hello World!" should print to the DOS window.

2.2   *Other Platforms*

Running Java programs under Unix is essentially the same as under Windows. There are different editors, and the command prompt is always available, but the steps are essentially the same. (Note that under Unix the directory separator is /, not \.)

For Macintosh, before Mac OS 10, it goes a little differently. We'll go through this assuming the SimpleText editor. First, double-click on the SimpleText icon. Then type in the program as above. Save the program in the File menu as HelloWorld.java. To compile the program into something the computer can understand, drag the newly created HelloWorld.java file onto the javac icon. This will create a new file HelloWorld.class. Finally, to run the program, drop the HelloWorld.class file on the JBindery icon.

2.3   Some Details

The procedure outlined above treats the Java language as a *compiled* language. That is, code is first converted into something the computer understands and is run later. It's actually a little more complex. Recall that compiled Java programs can be run on *any* computer. What this means is that compiling a Java program can't result in machine code, since machine code is specific to the kind of computer the program is being compiled on.

In point of fact, what happens with Java code is that javac compiles it into what's called **bytecode**. When java is invoked on the compiled **bytecode**, it does so by first creating a virtual computer: the **Java Virtual Machine** (JVM). The compiled bytecode is then run within this virtual computer. Thus, while Java code is indeed compiled, it's not compiled into machine code *per se*, but into bytecode, which runs on the JVM. The JVM is guaranteed to behave the same way on all platforms.

2.4   Summary

This chapter has introduced the basic edit–compile–run cycle for Java programming. First, you create your program in a text file. Then you compile your program into something the computer understands. Last, you run – or execute – your program.

2.5   Exercises

1. Change the text that's printed when HelloWorld is run.
2. Alter the HelloWorld program so that it prints two different things.
3. Take the HelloWorld program and rename it. This is actually trickier than it sounds; you have to do *two* different things here.

Note

[1] Depending on where you created myjava, you might have to cd further down in your directory structure; for example, cd \"My Documents"\myjava. (Notice how quotes are required when the directory name includes spaces.)

Chapter 3
The Basics

This chapter introduces the basic syntax of the Java™ programming language. The basic idea of a program as a sequence of operations is introduced. I also go through variables and data types. The chapter concludes with a presentation of control structures. Any program you could possibly write will need to use these, so this is essential information for any Java programmer.

These ideas are presented with very simple programs that don't do very much that's useful, but don't be misled. The concepts introduced in this chapter will form the heart of any program you write.

3.1   Comments and the Form of Programs

There are a number of things you should do when you program that are not strictly necessary to get the program to work, but that really help in understanding what you are doing and help you to avoid mistakes.

One very useful thing that you have seen already is using tabs and returns to indicate the structure of a program. The javac program doesn't care about tabs and line returns (except in strings), so we use these to make sure the structure and logic of a program is as apparent as possible.

A second very important thing to do is to put in **comments**. Comments are bits of text that javac doesn't see, but that help to remind the programmer what some bit of code is doing. This may seem silly at first, but is extremely helpful, especially when you're looking back at some big hunk of code you may no longer remember writing.

There are two kinds of comments, single- and multi-line. Single-line comments begin with the character sequence // and go to the end of the line. Multi-line comments begin with /* and end with */, and can go on for as many lines as necessary. Here is how the HelloWorld program looks when we add in a couple of comments:

```
public class HelloWorld {
    //This is the main group
    public static void main(String argv[]) {
        /* The following command looks pretty long and
        complicated, but it just prints something out. */
        System.out.println("Hello World!");
    }
}
```

The commented program compiles and runs just like the uncommented one.

3.2   *Variables*

One of the most useful concepts in programming is the **variable**. The idea is that information can be put into variables and then manipulated by other commands. Variables are rather like pronouns such as *it* or *them*, or deictics such as *this* or *that* in human language. Let's start with the simplest kinds of variables: **strings** and **integers**.

There are three parts to using a variable. First, it must be declared. That is, Java must be told that it exists, what kind of variable it is, and what its name is. For example, a string variable with the name hat and an integer variable with the name chair would be declared with the following statements:

```
String hat;
int chair;
```

Variable names must be composed of letters and numbers, and the first character must be a letter. Here, I've chosen hat and chair completely arbitrarily. Note incidentally that String is capitalized and int is not. This is actually critical, but let's leave off understanding why until later. By convention, Java programmers use lower-case letters for variable names, except to show word breaks; for example, myVariable or theNumber. The name can be anything you want, but it is best to name your variables mnemonically. For example, if you need a variable to store people's ages, name it age, rather than j. As with comments and indentation, this will help you keep track of what your program is doing.

The second part to using a variable is assigning it a value. In Java, this is done with the assignment operator =. For example, the variables above would be assigned "the purple house" and 13 respectively, as below:

```
hat = "the purple house";
chair = 13;
```

Notice that the string variable is surrounded with quotes.

It is possible to both declare and assign a variable in the same statement:

```
String hat = "the purple house";
int chair = 13;
```

I will avoid this as much as possible, so that these logically distinct functions are made as distinct as possible.

The third part is to use the variable. This is done by simply plugging the variable into a function where an argument would normally occur. The only function we have so far is System.out.println(), so let's try this out. The VblTest1 program shows how this works:[1]

```
public class VblTest1 {
    public static void main(String argv[]) {
        String hat;
        int chair;
        hat = "the purple house";
        System.out.println(hat);
        chair = 13;
        System.out.println(chair);
    }
}
```

First, as with the HelloWorld program, there is a group indicating that this is a program called VblTest1. Second, there is a group that indicates what the Java program is supposed to do first. Within that group, there are six statements, all properly terminated with semicolons. These are executed in sequence. The first two declare the variables hat and chair. The third assigns a value to the string variable hat, while the fourth executes the command System.out.println() on that variable, printing it. The fifth and sixth statements do the same with the integer variable chair. This program produces the following output:

```
> java VblTest1
the purple house
13

>
```

An important property of variables is that they can be reassigned. For example, the program VblTest2 shows how the same command has different results when reassignment occurs:

```
public class VblTest2 {
    public static void main(String argv[]) {
        String hat;
        hat = "the purple house";
        System.out.println(hat);
        hat = "the red chair";
        System.out.println(hat);
    }
}
```

First, a string variable hat is declared. Then it is assigned the value "the purple house". This variable is then printed, printing out "The purple house". Next, the same variable is assigned a *new* value "the red chair", and is printed again. The VblTest2 program produces the following output:

```
> java VblTest2
the purple house
the red chair

>
```

Notice how the second time hat is printed, its new value is printed, not the original one.

Let's now try some additional operations on variables. Integers can be manipulated with the usual numerical operations: +, -, *, /, %, and so on:

Operator	Meaning	Example
+	Addition	2 + 3 == 5
-	Subtraction	3 - 2 == 1
*	Multiplication	3 * 2 == 6
/	Division	6 / 2 == 3
%	Modulo	7 % 2 == 1

The program VblTest3 shows how these can be used:

```
public class VblTest3 {
    public static void main(String argv[]) {
        System.out.println(2 + 3);
        int chair;
        int stool;
        chair = 4;
        stool = 10;
        chair = chair * stool;
        System.out.println(chair);
```

```
        System.out.println(chair / 3);
        System.out.println(chair % 7);
    }
}
```

This program includes some tricky new stuff, so let's go through it step by step. As usual, there is an outermost class statement which must match the name of the file. Next, indented one layer, is the main group. This includes nine statements. The first statement prints out the result of adding 2 to 3. Notice how the arithmetic operation is thus performed *before* the printing takes place. The second and third statements declare two new variables, chair and stool, and the fourth and fifth statements assign values to them, of 4 and 10 respectively. The sixth statement looks quite odd until one remembers that = is assignment, not equals. The variable chair is assigned its own value – 4 – times the value of stool; that is, 40. The following statement then prints this out. The eighth statement prints out the result of dividing chair, 40, by 3. This produces the *integer* value 13. The final statement shows how the remainder of a division operation can be gotten with modulus, here 5.

The + operator can also be used with strings to indicate concatenation. This is demonstrated with VblTest4:

```
public class VblTest4 {
    public static void main(String argv[]) {
        String hat;
        hat = "This " + "is " + "a " + "long " + "string.";
        System.out.println(hat);
        hat = hat + " Uhoh!";
        System.out.println(hat);
        hat = "2" + "3";
        System.out.println(hat);
    }
}
```

This produces the output:

```
> java VblTest3
This is a long string.
This is a long string. Uhoh!
23

>
```

Notice that the last line of output is 23, not 5. The double quotes force "2" and "3" to be interpreted as strings by +. They are therefore concatenated, not added.

3.3 *Arrays*

It is sometimes convenient to group variables together, and this is what **arrays** are used for. An array is a finite sequence of variables of some particular type. For example, hat[] can be declared as a sequence of three integer variables and tomato[] as a sequence of 17 string variables. We might use the former to keep track of the sizes of different hats and the latter to keep track of the different names of tomato plants; for example, roma, cherry, pear, and so on:

```
int hat[] = new int[3];
String tomato[] = new String[17];
```

Notice the use of the keyword new to declare an array. This was not necessary in the case of simple variables. (We'll see new again when we take up objects in later chapters.)

Individual array members are referred to by number, *starting at zero*. Thus the three integer variables initialized for hat[] above are: hat[0], hat[1], and hat[2]. Once they've been declared, array values are assigned in the usual way, and used as expected. This is exemplified in ArrayTest, which simply prints out the contents of the array it creates:

```
public class ArrayTest {
    public static void main(String argv[]) {
        int hat[] = new int[3];
        hat[0] = 17;
        hat[1] = 0;
        hat[2] = 56;
        System.out.println(hat[2]);
        System.out.println(hat[1]);
        System.out.println(hat[0]);
    }
}
```

Notice that the order of array elements can be whatever you need. Here they are assigned in one order, and printed out in reverse order.

3.4 *Control Structures*

So far, we have treated a Java program as a sequence of statements, grouped together by the main group, within a larger group that defines the name of the program. In this section, we consider **control structures**. These provide lower-level grouping of statements. They allow statements to apply *conditionally*, and they can force changes in the otherwise top-down order that statements are executed in.

3.4.1   if/else

The most common control structure is the if/then or if/then/else structure. It comes in two flavors, with and without an **else-block**. Here is the simpler form:

```
if (if-clause) {
    any number of statements
}
```

I will refer to the statements bounded by the curly braces as the **then-block**. If the **if-clause** is true, then the statements in the then-block apply. (Note that the word *then* does not actually occur in the structure.) This structure can probably be best understood with an example:

```
public class IfExample {
    public static void main(String argv[]) {
        int myInt;
        myInt = 1;
        if (myInt > 2) {
            System.out.println("big");
        }
    }
}
```

In IfExample, the variable myInt is assigned a value and then there is an if/then test. If myInt is greater than two, the program prints the string big. Try changing the numerical assignments to myInt and recompiling to see how this works.

There are any number of tests for the if-clause within the Java language. Let's look at some of the ones for numbers first:

```
<     less than
>     greater than
<=    less than or equals
>=    greater than or equals
!=    not equals
==    equals
```

Notice especially that the symbol for equals is ==, not =. The latter is the assignment operator. To test for numerical equality, use ==. Mixing these up is an especially common error, so be careful to avoid it. Let's revise the above code to use more of these:

```
public class IfEx2 {
    public static void main(String argv[]) {
        int myInt;
        myInt = 1;
        if (myInt > 2) {
            System.out.println("big");
        }
        if (myInt <= 2) {
            System.out.println("small");
        }
    }
}
```

The IfEx2 program adds a second if/then structure. If myInt is greater than two, it prints out big; if it is smaller than or equal to two, it prints out small.
    This can be simplified by using an else-block. The schematic form is:

```
if (if-clause) {
    any number of statements
} else {
    any number of statements
}
```

I will refer to the set of statements after the else as the **else-block**. We can revise IfEx2 as IfEx3 using an else-block:

```
public class IfEx3 {
    public static void main(String argv[]) {
        int myInt;
        myInt = 1;
        if (myInt > 2) {
            System.out.println("big");
        } else {
            System.out.println("small");
        }
    }
}
```

This program prints out "big" if the number is greater than two, and "small" in all other cases; that is, when the number is less than or equal to two.
    In fact, one can have any number of if-clauses followed by at most one else-block. All the ifs except the first have a preceding else. The following program exemplifies:

```
public class IfEx4 {
    public static void main(String argv[]) {
        int myInt;
        myInt = 1;
        if (myInt > 2) {
            System.out.println("big");
        } else if ( myInt == 2) {
            System.out.println("2!");
        } else {
            System.out.println("small");
        }
    }
}
```

The IfEx4 program tests if myInt is greater than two, if it is equal to two, or if it is something else (less than two being the only remaining possibility).

String variables can also be tested in an if-clause, though the syntax is a little more complex. Here are the most useful tests (the examples in the table below assume that the String variable hat has been assigned the value "chair"):

Test	Function	Example	Explanation
String.equals()	Equality	hat.equals("chair")	Returns true or false
String.indexOf()	Substring	hat.indexOf("ha")	Returns an integer that indicates at what point in the string the argument begins at; Returns -1 if the argument is not a substring
String.length()	String length	hat.length()	Returns the number of characters in the string

To test for string-equality, one uses the String.equals() predicate; to test for inclusion, one uses the String.indexOf(); and to test for the length of a string, one uses String.length(). These have a different syntax because although strings look like integers, they are are actually **objects**, rather than basic data types like ints. (This distinction is treated in chapter 6.) The following sample code shows how the three string predicates work:

```
public class IfEx5 {
    public static void main(String argv[]) {
        String myString;
        myString = "this is a string";
        System.out.println(myString);
```

```
        if (myString.equals("this")) {
            System.out.println("myString equals \"this\".");
        } else if (myString.indexOf("this") > -1) {
            System.out.println("myString contains \"this\".");
        } else if (myString.length() > 10) {
            System.out.println("myString is really long: " +
                myString.length());
        }
    }
}
```

Let's look at the if-clauses first. The first if-clause checks whether myString is equal to the string "this". The second clause checks if myString contains "this". The way String.indexOf() works is that it returns an integer ranging from -1 to the length of the string (in terms of characters). If it returns -1, then the second string is not a substring of the first. If it returns something else, then the second string is a substring of the first. The particular number returned indicates where the substring begins counting from the left, starting at zero. Hence testing that String.indexOf() returns something greater than -1 amounts to checking if the second string is a substring of the first. Finally, the last if-clause above tests for the length of the string. In this case, it tests for whether the string is longer than ten characters.

Beware of common errors here. It will *not* work to use == with strings. Likewise, it will not work to use equals with integers. Note too that indexOf() and length() return integers that are then tested with the numerical tests already given. It may seem that the string tests are expressed rather strangely, but we'll see in chapter 6 that this syntax is quite sensible, and quite general.

There are two other things to notice about IfEx5. First, notice that since quotes are used to delimit strings, \" must be used to actually indicate the quote *character*. Also, notice the use of + in the last then-block. This statement prints out a string followed by the length of the string. The length of the string is computed by the length() command which is embedded in the print command. This kind of embedding is perfectly legal, but should be used cautiously. It can easily result in unreadable code. A more careful statement of this block would be as follows:

```
int myStrLength;
myStrLength = myString.length();
. . .
} else if (myStrLength > 10) {
    System.out.println("myString is really long: " + myStrLength);
}
. . .
```

In addition to being more readable, this snippet is actually more efficient, since the length of the string is only computed once and stored in the variable myStrLength.

The if/then control structure is quite powerful and allows for other possibilities as well. It allows for test conditions to be combined using the standard logical connectives:

```
&&   and
||   or
!    not
```

Here is an example:

```
public class IfEx6 {
    public static void main(String argv[]) {
        String myString;
        myString = "this is a string";
        int myInt;
        myInt = 5;
        if ((myInt > 4) && (myString.length() != 10)) {
            System.out.println("That worked!");
        }
    }
}
```

This tests if the integer is greater than four *and* if the length of the string is other than ten characters.

3.4.2   switch

The switch structure isn't really necessary, but it is used in some other programming languages and was included to make learning the Java language easier for programmers already familiar with the structure.[2] It has the following syntax:

```
switch(integer-variable) {
    case integer-value:
        any number of statements
        break;
    case integer-value:
        any number of statements
        break;
    case integer-value:
        any number of statements
        break;
```

```
  . . .
  default:
     any number of statements
}
```

There can be any number of case statements and at most one default statement. Each case statement is (generally) followed by a break. The basic idea is
that the value of the integer-variable determines which case applies. If no
specific case applies, then the default is applicable. Here's an example:

```
public class SwitchEx1 {
   public static void main(String argv[]) {
      int theInt;
      theInt = 5;
      switch(theInt) {
         case 2:
            System.out.println("That's a 2!");
            break;
         case 5:
            System.out.println("That's a 5.");
            break;
         default:
            System.out.println("What number was that?");
      }
   }
}
```

The SwitchEx1 program checks the value of theInt. If it is a two, it prints out
one thing, a five something else. Otherwise, it defaults to printing a third
statement.

Notice that the default-clause isn't required. If it's left out, then there is no
default case. If we remove the default-clause from SwitchEx1, then if theInt is
neither two nor five, nothing happens.

The break statements separate each case-clause from the next. If there is no
break between two case-clauses, then the first case "falls through" to the
next. That is, once the right case-clause is found, all statements that follow it
are executed until a break statement. This is exemplified in SwitchEx2:

```
public class SwitchEx2 {
   public static void main(String argv[]) {
      int theInt;
      theInt = 2;
      switch(theInt) {
         case 2:
            System.out.println("That's a 2!");
```

```
        case 5:
            System.out.println("That's a 5.");
            break;
        default:
            System.out.println("What number was that?");
    }
  }
}
```

The SwitchEx2 program differs from SwitchEx1 in two ways. First, theInt is initialized to 2. Second, the first break statement is removed. When theInt is checked for its value, case 2 is selected. However, since case 2 is not terminated by a break, the statement in case 5 is executed as well:

```
> java SwitchEx2
That's a 2!
That's a 5.

>
```

Here this is obviously not the behavior we want, but leaving out breaks judiciously can allow us to group case statements together in interesting ways.

There are two things to keep in mind about switch. First, it can *only* be used with integer values. Second, any switch statement can be replaced with some combination of if/then statements (which, as we have seen, are not restricted to tests for integer values).

3.4.3   while/do

The next two control structures – while/do and for – allow for iteration. They are very powerful, but it is quite easy to misuse them, ending up with an infinite loop, so some care must be taken when using them.

The syntax of while is straightforward:

```
while (while-condition) {
    any number of statements
}
```

As long as the while-condition is true, the statements in the main loop will repeat. It is therefore *essential* that you put in some sort of **exit condition**. If you don't, then the loop will iterate *forever*, which would be a problem if you ever want to use your computer again.

One very common strategy is to make some sort of counter, incrementing the counter with each iteration, and checking the value of the counter within the while-condition. The following program shows how this works:

```
public class WhileEx1 {
    public static void main(String argv[]) {
        int myInt;
        myInt = 0;
        while (myInt < 10) {
            System.out.println("myInt = " + myInt);
            myInt = myInt + 1;
        }
    }
}
```

This produces the following output:

```
> java WhileEx1
myInt = 0
myInt = 1
myInt = 2
myInt = 3
myInt = 4
myInt = 5
myInt = 6
myInt = 7
myInt = 8
myInt = 9

>
```

Let's examine how it works. First, the variable myInt is assigned the value zero. Then the while-condition is examined and satisfied. Then the print statement is executed and the value of myInt is incremented by one. (This kind of incrementing is so common that there is a special syntax for it: myInt++.) The while-condition is again examined and the body is again iterated through. This keeps happening until the while-condition is not true. At that point, the while structure is exited.

As I mentioned above, there are a number of errors that you can make with a while structure that have horrific consequences. For example, imagine you forgot to include the incrementing statement in WhileEx1. The while structure would loop forever. It would be a good idea not to do this.

There is a variant on the while structure called do/while. It has the following syntax:

```
do {
    any number of statements
} while (while-condition);
```

The structure differs from the simpler while structure in three ways. First, the while-condition *follows* the loop. This reflects the fact that the while-condition is assessed *after* the loop. Second, there is the keyword do at the beginning of the expression. Finally, there is a semicolon after the while-condition. Here is an example that produces the exact same output as WhileEx1:

```
public class WhileEx2 {
    public static void main(String argv[]) {
        int myInt;
        myInt = 0;
        do {
            System.out.println("myInt = " + myInt);
            myInt = myInt + 1;
        } while (myInt < 10);
    }
}
```

It's possible for the two structures to have different consequences, however. Consider the following two examples:

```
public class WhileEx3 {
    public static void main(String argv[]) {
        int myInt;
        myInt = 0;
        while (myInt < 0) {
            System.out.println("myInt = " + myInt);
            myInt = myInt + 1;
        }
    }
}
```

```
public class WhileEx4 {
    public static void main(String argv[]) {
        int myInt;
        myInt = 0;
        do {
            System.out.println("myInt = " + myInt);
            myInt = myInt + 1;
        } while (myInt < 0);
    }
}
```

I leave it as an exercise (3.2 below) to explain why these have different outputs.

There are many other ways to use a while/do structure beyond overtly incrementing a counter. We will see many more examples of this useful device in the chapters that follow. For now, I give just one. The Java language supplies a command System.currentTimeMillis() which returns a representation of the current time in milliseconds. We can use this to demonstrate the extra power of the while/do structure. The System.currentTimeMillis() command returns a number that is too big to be represented as an int. Java allows for this and has a data type long for holding bigger numbers. The following code makes use of while/do to wait a specified number of milliseconds:

```
public class WhileEx5 {
    public static void main(String argv[]) {
        long waitTime, firstTime, secondTime, diffTime;
        waitTime = 2000;
        diffTime = 0;
        System.out.println("starting...");
        firstTime = System.currentTimeMillis();
        while (diffTime < waitTime) {
            secondTime = System.currentTimeMillis();
            diffTime = secondTime - firstTime;
        }
        System.out.println("wait time was: " + diffTime);
    }
}
```

The program first declares several long variables in a *single* statement. It then initializes two of them and prints a little message. The program collects the current time as firstTime. The while-loop gathers the (now) current time, storing it as secondTime. The second statement of the while-loop computes the difference between the two times. The while-condition tests whether the difference between the two times is still less than the predefined waiting time of 2000 milliseconds. Notice that this loop is also based on a counter, time, but a counter that is incremented independently of the program.

3.4.4   for

The for control structure also allows for iteration and builds in an explicit counter. The syntax is as follows:

```
for (base-case; test-case; increment-case) {
    any number of statements
}
```

The base-case defines a counter and sets the value at which it starts. The test-case tells the Java program when to stop looping. The increment-case indicates how the counter is altered at each loop. Here's a simple example:

```
public class ForEx1 {
   public static void main(String argv[]) {
      for (int i = 0; i < 10; i++) {
         System.out.println("the value of i is " + i);
      }
   }
}
```

Here a counter i is defined as an int and assigned the initial value of 0. The test is whether i remains less than 10. Each time through the loop, i is incremented by one. This program produces the same output as WhileEx1 and WhileEx2.

The change in the value of i does not have to be an increment. Any other regular mathematical relationship is legal as well. For example, we could do the whole thing by *decrementing* i instead, as in ForEx2 below:

```
public class ForEx2 {
   public static void main(String argv[]) {
      for (int i = 10; i > 0; i--) {
         System.out.println("the value of i is " + i);
      }
   }
}
```

Notice that i-- is an abbreviation for i = i - 1, just as i++ is an abbreviation for i = i + 1.

Anything that can be done with a for can also be done with a while. The advantage of for is that it forces you to program the exit condition and increment/decrement up front, which helps to avoid errors.

3.4.5   try/catch

The final control structure that we consider is try/catch. The basic syntax is as follows:

```
try {
   any number of statements
} catch (Exception e) {
   any number of statements
}
```

Certain operations in any programming language are prone to error. These are typically those that involve accessing computer resources beyond simple processing and writing to the screen. For example, reading a file might result in the file not being where it should be, or the contents not being as expected. Making a network connection may not be possible at a given time.

Java commands of this sort are set up so that when an error of this type is possible, the language *requires* you to write code that can handle the situation. For example, if you want to write a program that opens a file, then you are required to write code for what happens if the file isn't found or can't be opened.

Such commands are said to "throw an exception" when they generate one of these possible errors. When you write code that deals with such an error – the exception – your code is "catching the exception".

Let's take the case of opening a file and show how this works schematically. Imagine that all you want is for your program to print out a reasonable error message if the file isn't found. This would be handled schematically as follows:

```
try {
    statements that open a file and throw a FileNotFoundException
} catch (FileNotFoundException e) {
    System.out.println("Oops! The file was missing.");
}
```

An example of a fairly simple command that requires a try/catch structure is the Thread.sleep() command. This command forces the program to halt for the specified number of milliseconds. Here is a simple example:

```
public class Try1 {
    public static void main(String argv[]) {
        System.out.println("starting...");
        try {
            Thread.sleep(2000);
        } catch (InterruptedException e) {
            System.out.println("Oops!");
        }
        System.out.println("Time's up!");
    }
}
```

If the Thread.sleep() command has a problem and throws an exception, then the catch-clause is invoked, printing the very useful error message "Oops!".

You can see yourself that the Thread.sleep() command requires a try/catch structure if you try to compile the incorrect TryWRONG program below:

```
public class TryWRONG {
    public static void main(String argv[]) {
```

```
        System.out.println("starting...");
        Thread.sleep(2000);
        System.out.println("Time's up!");
    }
}
```

The javac compiler issues an error message saying that Thread.sleep() throws an InterruptedException that must be caught.[3]

3.5   *Experimental Stimuli*

We don't really have enough yet to do very substantive programs, but we do have just enough to show how programming can already help the language researcher. In this section, we develop a small program to create experimental stimuli.

Imagine you are a syntactician interested in the grammaticality of sentences such as "John and Mary see Gretchen". For some reason, you think the choice of names might affect what people think the final sentence means. To this end, you have some number of names, say seven, and some number of verbs, say three, and you want to create all possible combinations to test your theory.

If you've worked out the math, you'll see that there are 1,029 combinations ($7 \cdot 7 \cdot 3 \cdot 7 = 1,029$), a rather tedious job.[4]

This is actually quite easy to do in the Java programming language. First, we define two String arrays, one to contain the names, and the other to contain the verbs. We then use nested for loops to combine every possible combination in the following template: "NAME and NAME VERB NAME". A program doing this is given below. Notice how we've used a new convenient syntax to declare and assign all the elements of an array in one step:

```
public class Stimuli1 {
    public static void main(String argv[]) {
        String names[] = {"Mike", "Joe", "Diane", "Puck", "Artie", "Sunny",
            "Bob"};
        String verbs[] = {"see", "chase", "have fun with"};
        for (int i = 0; i < names.length; i++) {
            for (int j = 0; j < names.length; j++) {
                for (int k = 0; k < verbs.length; k++) {
                    for (int m = 0; m < names.length; m++) {
                        System.out.println(names[i] + " and " +
                            names[j] + " " + verbs[k] + " " +
                            names[m]);
                    }
```

```
                    }
                  }
                }
              }
            }
```

The nesting allows for all combinations in the four positions, printing out all 1,029 combinations.

Now imagine that, having watched this huge list scroll by, it's apparent that we don't want our list to contain any repeated names; that is, we don't want sentences such as "Mike and Joe see Joe". This is quite easily done by embedding an if-clause above the print method and below the nested for-loops that tests for identity among the nouns. This is done by checking if any of the array indices for names are the same:

```java
public class Stimuli2 {
    public static void main(String argv[]) {
        String names[] = {"Mike", "Joe", "Diane", "Puck",
            "Artie", "Sunny", "Bob"};
        String verbs[] = {"see", "chase", "have fun with"};
        for (int i = 0; i < names.length; i++) {
            for (int j = 0; j < names.length; j++) {
                for (int k = 0; k < verbs.length; k++) {
                    for (int m = 0; m < names.length; m++) {
                        if ((i != j) && (i != m) && (j != m)) {
                            System.out.println(names[i] + " and " +
                                names[j] + " " + verbs[k] + " " +
                                names[m]);
                        }
                    }
                }
            }
        }
    }
}
```

This produces 630 sentences ($7 \cdot 6 \cdot 3 \cdot 5 = 630$).

3.6 *Summary*

This chapter has introduced the basic syntax of the Java language. This is really the heart of the language; all the rest is really icing on this cake. Variables and arrays allow us to store information and manipulate it later with functions provided by Java technology (or ones that you write yourself). Control structures allow us to adjust the way in which the Java language executes the commands of your program, branching and looping as you need.

3.7   Exercises

1. Why do the following behave differently: 1 + 2 versus "1" + "2"?
2. Why do WhileEx3 and WhileEx4 have different outputs?
3. Rewrite SwitchEx1 using the if/then structure.
4. Write a program that has the following properties. It uses an array of strings to store six names. Then it uses a for structure to iterate through the array, printing each name. Finally, the for-loop should have only one statement in it.
5. Write a program that exemplifies putting an if/then structure *inside* a while structure.
6. How would you find out how many iterations does the loop in WhileEx5 go through to reach 2,000 milliseconds? Alter the code slightly to collect this information.

Notes

[1] Remember from chapter 2 how to create a program like this one, named VblTest1. It must be put in a text file with the name VblTest1.java.
[2] I include it for completeness, and will avoid it almost totally in subsequent chapters.
[3] There are more complications to the try/catch structure, but I leave them to more advanced texts, since they are irrelevant to our goals.
[4] Once you've got them all, its rather a nightmare to imagine how you might test your theory on human beings, but let's leave that aside for now . . .

Chapter 4
Input and Output

We have seen that Java™ programs are created in text files with the extension ".java". When we run the Java compiler javac, this creates a corresponding ".class" file which can be run by the JVM using the java command. Java programs can manipulate files as well. In this chapter, I present the Java **input–output** (IO) system. IO is necessary for your programs to interact with the world, for them to do any useful work.

4.1   Reading and Writing

The Java syntax that we went through in the previous chapter is quite powerful, but is not really much use yet. So far, all we can do is print things to the screen. To really make variables, arrays, and control structures do some work, we need to allow the Java language to *interact* with the outside world in some way. For our purposes, this means to interact with language data. Those data can either come from files or from human subjects.

Getting data to and from these different sources means using the Java IO system. The full IO system is *incredibly* complicated and I will *not* go through the whole thing. It's complex for three reasons.

First, the IO system allows one to read many different kinds of data from many different sources (and write the same types back to the same places). In this book, I focus on textual language data but, even from a linguistic point of view, we might also want to go on to consider, say, raw acoustic data.

Another source of complexity is that the Java IO system is set up so that data can be manipulated and filtered as it is read and written. A relatively simple example of this is data compression, such as zipped or gzipped files. (There's an example of this in this chapter.) There are Java utility IO routines that handle these straightforwardly.

Finally, Java IO is complicated because of **internationalization**. The idea is that not only should Java code be able to be run on any type of computer, but it should run properly no matter what the conventions are of the country that the computer is in. What this means is that if you have a program that, say, prints out the date, then if you do things properly and take full advantage of the internationalization routines, you should be able to have the date display in the appropriate language and appropriate format for whatever country your user is in.

There are five input–output conditions that I will go over:

Input	Output
Prompt	Prompt
File	File
Command line	

The input cases I treat are command-line input, reading from the prompt, and reading from a file. The output cases are writing to the prompt and writing to a file.

I have, in fact, already covered writing to the prompt. The command System.out.println() allows us to print output to the system prompt. I should note here, though, that the notion of system prompt has to be understood generously. Macintoshes don't have a system prompt. When Java commands that refer to the prompt are invoked on a Mac, the Java technology creates a special window for them.[1]

4.2   Command-Line Input

Command-line input refers to the possibility of typing in arguments to a program as you type in the command to run the program. For example, in Windows and Unix, the commands java and javac themselves take the names of files as command-line arguments. (As with the system prompt, this has to be understood differently on a Mac. Program names cannot be typed in anywhere on a Mac, and so there is no general arrangement for command-line input. Whenever a Java program is invoked on a Mac, the Java technology creates a small window and asks the user for any command-line arguments.)

While we have not made use of this option yet, all of the programs we have written have in fact made allowance for command-line input. Recall the loop that instructs the Java code what to do first when a program is run:

```
public static void main(String argv[]) {
   . . .
}
```

This group includes a reference to what appears to be an array of strings: argv[]. This array of strings, in fact, contains any terms that are entered on the command line when the program is typed in. For example, if you had run a program called myprog and invoked it as below, then the terms "33" and "hats" would be available to the program as argv[0] and argv[1] respectively:

```
java myprog 33 hats
```

Here's a program that exemplifies this:

```
public class CLEx1 {
   public static void main(String argv[]) {
      System.out.println(argv[0]);
   }
}
```

If you invoke CLEx1 with a command-line argument, it prints it out. Notice what happens, though, if you invoke it with no command-line argument. The JVM produces an error: ArrayIndexOutOfBoundsException. Basically, if there is no command-line argument, then the array argv[] has no elements. The error comes from the fact that the program attempts to print the first member of an array that has nothing in it.

There are several ways to deal with this. One possibility would be to make use of the try/catch control structure introduced in the preceding chapter. We could explicitly deal with the possibility that the user might enter no command-line argument:

```
public class CLEx2 {
   public static void main(String argv[]) {
      try {
         System.out.println(argv[0]);
      } catch (ArrayIndexOutOfBoundsException e) {
         System.out.println("Enter an argument on the command-line.");
      }
   }
}
```

Entering CLEx2 with an argument prints the argument. Entering it without an argument prints the complaint in the catch-clause.

While this is an improvement, we can do even better. Notice that if you supply *two* command-line arguments, only the first will be printed. Here is a revision of the program that prints any number of arguments:

```
public class CLEx3 {
   public static void main(String argv[]) {
      for (int i = 0; i < argv.length; i++) {
         System.out.println(argv[i]);
      }
   }
}
```

This program prints out the command-line arguments one at a time. It makes use of one new bit of code. The size of any array, arrayname, is stored in an integer variable called arrayname.length. Thus the number of command-line arguments is stored in argv.length. Notice that this integer *variable* is different from the *command* for determining the number of characters in a string: String.length(). It is very easy to mix these up, so be careful.

One last thing to note about command-line arguments is that the Java language treats them as strings. This means that you need to do something special if you want to treat them as numbers, say, if you want to do arithmetic on them. Imagine you want to write a program that adds together any numbers given it on the command line, and then prints out the result. The problem is that the Java language will not allow you to add strings together. (In fact, as we saw in the preceding chapter, the Java language will interpret + with respect to strings as concatenation, rather than addition.) To avoid this, we must *convert* each command-line argument to an integer before doing addition. The relevant command is Integer.parseInt() and is exemplified in CLEx4:

```
public class CLEx4 {
   public static void main(String argv[]) {
      int total, current;
      total = 0;
      for (int i = 0; i < argv.length; i++) {
         current = Integer.parseInt(argv[i]);
         total = total + current;
      }
      System.out.println("total: " + total);
   }
}
```

The Integer.parseInt() command will throw an exception if its argument is not something that can be converted to a number. I leave treatment of this as an exercise.

4.3   *The Java IO Model*

The Java IO system is built out of **streams**. For example, System.out is a stream that can be printed to. Likewise, there is a System.in which can be read from. Reading data from streams is done with **readers**, and writing to streams is done with **writers**. There are a huge number of streams, readers, and writers for various specialized purposes, but we will only treat the ones that we need.

4.3.1   The prompt

We've already seen how to print to the screen with System.out.println(). Reading from the prompt requires a little more work.[2] There are three things that we need. First, data entered at the prompt comes in through the System.in stream and needs to be read by a basic reader. Second, if we want to read a *line* of text entered at the prompt, we have to invoke a special reader – BufferedReader – to do so. Finally, printing is handled asynchronously. That is, printing doesn't necessarily happen precisely when the printing instruction is given. To force it to do so, we need to "flush" the stream. Sample code exemplifying all this is given in PromptEx1:

```
public class PromptEx1 {
    public static void main(String argv[]) {
        System.out.println("Enter a line of text:");
        System.out.flush();
        String theInput = "";
        java.io.InputStreamReader isr =
            new java.io.InputStreamReader(System.in);
        java.io.BufferedReader br =
            new java.io.BufferedReader(isr);
        try {
            theInput = br.readLine();
            br.close();
        } catch (java.io.IOException e) {
            System.out.println("A problem occurred!");
        }
        System.out.println("You entered: " + theInput);
    }
}
```

There's a lot here, so let's go through this slowly. First, the program prints out a line of text that invites the user to enter text. This is followed by a command System.out.flush(), that flushes the System.out stream, forcing the printing to take place before continuing. Next, there is a line of code that declares a string variable theInput and initializes it to an empty string. The initializing isn't strictly necessary, but avoids an annoying warning by javac that theInput might not be initialized. This is because of the try/catch loop that follows.

Next, there are several mysterious statements. Readers and writers are **objects**, like strings. The following chapter treats objects in depth. For now, we need only think of them as *things*, things that have to be overtly created before they can be used. The first statement here declares and initializes an InputStreamReader that reads input from the keyboard (System.in). This reader is given the name isr. The next line of code declares and initializes a BufferedReader, which will allow us to read input a line at a time.

Notice that the names of these readers are quite long and are both prefaced with the string java.io. This is because IO is handled by special objects and routines that are not part of the basic Java language, but are part of the IO **package**. We'll see below that these long names can be shortened, but we won't do that yet.

Next, there is a try/catch loop. This is because reading from input throws an exception that must be caught. Notice that after input is read, we explicitly close the input stream. The command to close the input stream also throws an exception, so we've tucked it into the same try/catch expression.

This may seem like a lot of work to print out a line of text, but recall that the richness of the IO system allows for all sorts of power. At this point, the simplest thing is probably to treat the commands for prompt input as an idiom. Let's review the essential bits:

1   Create an InputStreamReader with the stream System.in.
2   Create a BufferedReader on top of the InputStreamReader.
3   In a try/catch loop, use the command readLine(), and then close() to close the input stream.

As you become an ever more sophisticated Java programmer, just why these steps are required will make more sense. At the beginning, it may be easier to simply memorize that these three steps are required.

Let's now simplify the code of PromptEx1 a little. First, let's arrange for the input to be typed on the same line as the instruction to enter the input. This is easily done by replacing System.out.println() with System.out.print(). The latter prints a line of text, but does not go on to the next line.

Second, let's eliminate all the java.io prefixes. This can be done by explicitly telling the compiler that we will be using machinery from the IO package. This is done with the import command, as in PromptEx2 below:

```
import java.io.*;

public class PromptEx2 {
    public static void main(String argv[]) {
        System.out.print("Enter a line of text: ");
        System.out.flush();
        String theInput = "";
        InputStreamReader isr = new InputStreamReader(System.in);
        BufferedReader br = new BufferedReader(isr);
        try {
            theInput = br.readLine();
            br.close();
        } catch (IOException e) {
            System.out.println("A problem occurred!");
        }
        System.out.println("You entered: " + theInput);
    }
}
```

The import command doesn't alter how the program works, but makes it easier to read and type!

4.3.2   File IO

Let's now consider file input and output. I'll treat the output case first, as that allows us to create some files to work with. Note that, in principle, writing to a file is a *risky undertaking*. You must make very sure that the filename you use is not already in use by some other file, else you run the risk of overwriting the existing file and deleting its contents. I would recommend creating a new directory and doing all your IO experimenting there, so as to minimize the risk.

To write output to a file, we must first make a connection to a file with a FileWriter object. This in turn is the basis for a BufferedWriter object, since we'll be writing line by line. Finally, we need a PrintWriter object to do the actual writing. These objects will need to be closed when we're done, and creating the FileWriter, writing to the file, and closing it all throw exceptions, so we'll need a try/catch loop. The FileEx1 program exemplifies these bits:

```
import java.io.*;

public class FileEx1 {
    public static void main(String argv[]) {
        try {
            FileWriter fw = new FileWriter("mh.txt");
            BufferedWriter bw = new BufferedWriter(fw);
```

```
        PrintWriter pw = new PrintWriter(bw);
        pw.println("This is a test.");
        pw.flush();
        fw.close();
    } catch (IOException e) {
        System.out.println("Something went wrong!");
    }
  }
}
```

This program creates a new file called mh.txt and writes a simple sentence to it.[3]

Reading from a file is, in fact, even easier. One creates a FileReader and then uses it to create a BufferedReader. The readers must be closed and all of that put in a try/catch loop. The following example shows how this works; it reads the contents of a file and prints them at the prompt. The only new part is reading line by line. What we want is to use the readLine() command line by line until the end of the file. We detect the end of the file by waiting with a while structure for readLine() to return a null:

```
import java.io.*;

public class FileEx2 {
    public static void main(String argv[]) {
        String line = "";
        try {
            FileReader fr = new FileReader("mh.txt");
            BufferedReader br = new BufferedReader(fr);
            while ((line = br.readLine()) != null) {
                System.out.println(line);
            }
            fr.close();
        } catch (IOException e) {
            System.out.println("Something went wrong!");
        }
    }
}
```

First, we declare and initialize a string variable line. We next create the readers that we need. The following while structure is the guts of the program. The program prints out the contents of line as long as the while-condition remains true. The while-condition tests whether line is successfully assigned the results of readLine(). If the end of the file is reached, assigning line the results of readLine() fails. The while-condition is then no longer true, and the while structure is exited. The while-condition is interesting because it's really doing *two* things at once. It's reading a line from the file into line, and it's testing whether that is successful.

4.3.3   Compression

As a final example of IO, let's go through how to do file compression. The Java language actually includes methods for both **zip** and **gzip** compression. We'll go over gzip compression. If you're unfamiliar with this, gzip compression is a method for making files smaller. It's quite useful when space is at a premium; for example, when downloading or emailing large files.

The Java language implements gzip compression as one more intermediary possibility in the IO system. The following program for compressing text shows how it works. There are two things to note at the outset. First, note the presence of the GZIPOutputStream object. Second, note that since gzip compression creates *binary* as opposed to text files, we need to convert from a text-based writer to a binary FileOutputStream:

```java
import java.io.*;
import java.util.zip.*;

public class FileEx3 {
    public static void main(String argv[]) {
        try {
            FileOutputStream fos = new FileOutputStream("mh.gz");
            GZIPOutputStream gos = new GZIPOutputStream(fos);
            OutputStreamWriter osw = new OutputStreamWriter(gos);
            BufferedWriter bw = new BufferedWriter(osw);
            PrintWriter pw = new PrintWriter(bw);
            pw.println("This is a test");
            pw.flush();
            pw.close();
        } catch (IOException e) {
            System.out.println(e.getMessage());
        }
    }
}
```

The gzip objects are actually part of the java.util.zip package, and so we need to include a new import statement. First, we create a FileOutputStream, allowing us to write binary data to a file mh.gz. The next step is to create the GZIPOutputStream, which will do the compression. Third, we create an OutputStreamWriter, which converts from characters to binary data. The remainder of the program is just like FileEx1. Note that we have departed from our usual exception-catching strategy; here we use the command e.getMessage(), which produces an informative statement about what exception was actually caught.

If you have decompression software on your computer, you can open the mh.gz file with it to see that it is indeed compressed in gzip format. However, the Java language also provides for a GZIPInputStream object to decompress files, which is exemplified in FileEx4 below:

```java
import java.io.*;
import java.util.zip.*;

public class FileEx4 {
    public static void main(String argv[]) {
        String line = "";
        try {
            FileInputStream fis = new FileInputStream("mh.gz");
            GZIPInputStream gis = new GZIPInputStream(fis);
            InputStreamReader isr = new InputStreamReader(gis);
            BufferedReader br = new BufferedReader(isr);
            while ((line = br.readLine()) != null) {
                System.out.println(line);
            }
            br.close();
        } catch (IOException e) {
            System.out.println(e.getMessage());
        }
    }
}
```

This program opens the gzipped file and converts it back into text which is printed to the screen. The code is rather self-explanatory. Since the gzipped file is binary data, we need a FileInputStream to read it. Since the binary data is compressed, we use a GZIPInputStream to decompress it. Since we know the compressed data is text and we want to deal with it as text, we use an InputStreamReader to convert the binary data to text. Finally, we use a BufferedReader to read the converted text line by line.

It's really only with programs such as FileEx3 and FileEx4 that the full elegance of the Java IO system comes out. We can nest these various streams, readers, and writers to achieve very powerful effects. Much much more is possible than I've shown here, but for language purposes, we don't need any more than what we have now.

4.4   *Pure Java Programming*

In this chapter I've covered some of the more useful Java IO methods. This will prove very useful in developing some very convenient utilities for linguistic research.

I should acknowledge, though, that some of the IO techniques explained here would greatly offend the Java purist. As noted above, the notion of a "prompt" is alien for some computer architectures, notably Macs. While Java technology running on a Mac can deal with all the examples that we've gone through, it doesn't handle them in a very natural fashion with respect to the Mac operating system. We will rectify this in later chapters when we deal with the **user interface**, but for now we'll have to live with this inelegance for pedagogical purposes.

4.5   *Summary*

This chapter has introduced the basic input–output options for the Java language: file, prompt, and command-line input, and file and prompt output.

The Java machinery for IO is rather complex, but extremely powerful and versatile. Moreover, we will see in subsequent chapters that IO is even more complex with a graphical user interface.

4.6   *Exercises*

1.   Revise CLEx4 so that if the user enters something that isn't a number and the Integer.parseInt() command throws an exception, then an appropriate error message is generated.
2.   Write a program that will display the contents of any text file to the screen. (This is the equivalent of Unix cat or DOS type.)
3.   I noted above that the Integer.parseInt() command will generate an exception if it is applied to something that can't be converted into an integer. Write a program that takes some number of command-line arguments and multiplies them together. Write the code necessary so that if the user should enter a nonnumerical argument, an appropriate error message will be displayed.
4.   Write a program that will take all the command-line arguments and put them in a text file, and simultaneously put them in a separate gzipped file.
5.   Alter the program that you wrote for the preceding exercise so that the file names are provided on the command line. (Make sure your program has the proper extensions for a text file (.txt) and a gzipped file (.gz).)

Notes

[1] A more traditional – and correct – term for this is **console**, not prompt. I use the latter in deference to my students, who objected strenuously to the former!

[2] Before Mac OS 10, to read from the prompt on a Mac, you must make sure that you've selected "redirect stdin from Message Window" in JBindery.

[3] As a precaution, I often use my own initials in naming files and variables. It's a convenient habit that avoids unfortunate accidents, as important system files and variables are rarely prefixed with my own initials.

Chapter 5
Methods

This chapter amplifies on the preceding one. I present the idea of **methods** and **return types**. These are needed to develop Java™ programs of any significant complexity. In the process, we develop a program for searching text files: DumbGrep.

5.1 Methods and Return Types

The programs we have written so far have been written as one huge block. The only internal organization we have used is that forced by the control structures that we've used. However, it is sometimes useful to impose additional structure. We can do this by means of **methods** or **subroutines**. Methods enable us to separate our programs into sensible and reusable modules. The basic idea is to define some new command composed of some series of existing commands. This new command can simply perform some action or series of actions, or it can return some sort of object; for example, an integer or string.

The syntax of a method is simple. If the method performs some sort of action, then it is defined as a group, just like main, but with some other name. This is exemplified in Meth1 below:

```
public class Meth1 {
    public static void main(String argv[]) {
        test();
    }
    public static void test() {
        System.out.println("This is a test.");
    }
}
```

The method is called test() and it simply prints out a string. It is defined with the same keywords as the main loop. Unlike the main part of the program, it takes no arguments and is therefore followed by empty parentheses in its definition. The method is called by the statement test(), again with empty parentheses. The method test() is not very useful, as it only contains a single statement, but let's get the general idea before doing some work with it.

Methods can also take arguments. For example, we can minimally modify Meth1 as Meth2 to show how this works:

```
public class Meth2 {
    public static void main(String argv[]) {
        test("1");
        test("2");
    }
    public static void test(String s) {
        System.out.println("This is test number " + s);
    }
}
```

Here the test() method is defined to take a string argument. In the definition of the method, the argument type and name is given in the parentheses following the method name. The argument name can then be invoked in the method definition. In this case, the string argument s is appended on the end of the string that is printed. Notice that, in this case, the test() method is invoked twice with different arguments. Again, the example is trivial, but the fact that the method can behave differently with different arguments gives a hint as to the power methods provide.

Methods can obviously be given integer arguments as well, but can be given any number of arguments too. The next program shows how this works:

```
public class Meth3 {
    public static void main(String argv[]) {
        test(3,"Mike");
    }
    public static void test(int n, String s) {
        for (int i = 0; i < n; i++) {
            System.out.println("Hello, " + s);
        }
    }
}
```

This program gives an integer and string argument to the revised test method, which prints out a new string the number of times indicated.

Methods can return objects as well; for example, strings and integers. Here is a rather silly example with a method that returns an integer:

```
public class Meth4 {
    public static void main(String argv[]) {
        int n,m;
        n = Integer.parseInt(argv[0]);
        m = timesThirtySeven(n);
        System.out.println("The result is: " + m);
    }
    public static int timesThirtySeven(int k) {
        return k * 37;
    }
}
```

The program defines two integers n and m, and the first is assigned the command-line argument. (Note, of course, that an error will result if no command-line argument is given, or if an argument is given that cannot be converted into an integer.) The integer m is assigned the result of applying the method timesThirtySeven() to n. The new method timesThirtySeven() is defined as returning an int in its declaration. The method body must then include the keyword return, which gives the value that the method calculates. Thus a method can be defined as void, returning nothing, or can be defined as returning something – for example, int – in which case it must contain a return statement.

Finally, here is a method that takes a string and returns a string:

```
public class Meth5 {
    public static void main(String argv[]) {
        for (int i = 0; i < argv.length; i++) {
            System.out.println(repeater(argv[i]));
        }
    }
    public static String repeater(String s) {
        return s + " " + s;
    }
}
```

This program simply takes the command-line arguments and prints each one out twice.

5.2   *Searching a Text File*

Let's now start to build some more substantive – and more useful – programs. In this section, we develop a program that will search through a file, printing out all lines that contain some particular pattern. We call this program DumbGrep (after the Unix utility grep). Let's have the pattern and the filename both being entered on the command line. The logic of the program is fairly straightforward using the programming tools we have developed so far. First, we use argv[] to read in the search pattern and the filename. Then we use a FileReader and a BufferedReader to make the appropriate connection to the file we want to read from. We use the usual while structure to loop through the file, and we use String.indexOf() to find lines that contain the pattern:

```java
import java.io.*;

public class DumbGrep1 {
    public static void main(String argv[]) {
        String word = argv[0];
        String filename = argv[1];
        String line;
        try {
            FileReader fr = new FileReader(filename);
            BufferedReader br = new BufferedReader(fr);
            while ((line = br.readLine()) != null) {
                if (line.indexOf(word) > -1) {
                    System.out.println(line);
                }
            }
            fr.close();
        } catch (Exception e) {
            System.out.println("Uhoh!");
        }
    }
}
```

Anticipating our further development of DumbGrep, let's put the actual search into a separate method. This is done in DumbGrep2:

```java
import java.io.*;

public class DumbGrep2 {
    public static void main(String argv[]) {
        String word = argv[0];
        String filename = argv[1];
        String line;
        try {
            FileReader fr = new FileReader(filename);
            BufferedReader br = new BufferedReader(fr);
```

```
            while ((line = br.readLine()) != null) {
                // findIt() is defined below
                if (findIt(line,word)) {
                    System.out.println(line);
                }
            }
            fr.close();
        } catch (Exception e) {
            System.out.println("Uhoh!");
        }
    }
    // this method does the search
    public static boolean findIt(String theLine, String theWord) {
        if (theLine.indexOf(theWord) > -1) {
            return true;
        } else {
            return false;
        }
    }
}
```

I have replaced the if-clause in DumbGrep1 with a new method in DumbGrep2. This new method is called findIt(). It takes two string arguments and is defined as returning something called a boolean. The boolean designation means that the method must return true or false. While DumbGrep2 doesn't do anything more than DumbGrep1, it provides us a convenient framework to develop the capabilities of the search component of the program: findIt().

Let's imagine that we want to allow the program to print out lines that match the pattern only at the beginning of a line or at the end of the line. We'll do this in stages. First, let's allow for matching either at the beginning of the line or anywhere in the line. We'll do this by adding a third optional command-line argument. If there is a third argument – and it is the word initial – then the match must be at the beginning of the line. To search for the string hat in a file myfile at the beginning of a line, one would type the following: java DumbGrep3 hat myfile initial.

Here's the code:

```
import java.io.*;

public class DumbGrep3 {
    public static void main(String argv[]) {
        String word = argv[0];
        String filename = argv[1];
        String optThird = "not";
        if (argv.length == 3) {
```

```
            optThird = argv[2];
        }
        // what if the user enters something else?
        if (!optThird.equals("initial")) {
            optThird = "not";
        }
        String line;
        try {
            FileReader fr = new FileReader(filename);
            BufferedReader br = new BufferedReader(fr);
            while ((line = br.readLine()) != null) {
                // findIt() defined below
                if (findIt(line,word,optThird)) {
                    System.out.println(line);
                }
            }
            fr.close();
        } catch (Exception e) {
            System.out.println("Uhoh!");
        }
    }
    // our own search method
    public static boolean findIt(String theLine,
            String theWord, String third) {
        // beginning of line
        if (third.equals("initial")) {
            if (theLine.indexOf(theWord) == 0) {
                return true;
            }
        // elsewhere
        } else {
            if (theLine.indexOf(theWord) > -1) {
                return true;
            }
        }
        return false;
    }
}
```

We've added a few lines at the beginning to parse the command-line arguments. If there are less than two arguments – or if the second argument is not a file that can be opened – the program will generate errors. A new string optThird is declared. If there is a third command-line argument and it is the word initial, then that is assigned to optThird. If not, then optThird is assigned the string not. The optThird string is passed as an argument to findIt(). The latter then returns a match differently depending on whether the match must be initial.

This does the trick, but is rather clumsy. A more elegant treatment is to alter the search string to trigger the behavior we want. First, let's invent some specialized terminology. We'll let ^ indicate the beginning of a line and $ indicate the end of a line.[1] Thus, if we enter hat as the pattern, a line matches if it contains "hat" anywhere. On the other hand, if we enter ^hat, then a match occurs only if the line begins with "hat". Entering ^hat$ generates a match only if the line is exactly "hat".

To make use of this, I make use of a new command String.substring(). This command returns a substring of the initial string bounded by its two integer arguments. For example, if the string variable hat is assigned the string "banana", then the command hat.substring(2,4) returns "na". What we'll do is keep the findIt() method from DumbGrep3, and add two new methods to parse off any potential ^ and set the value of optThird. The main method is slightly changed to refer to the two new methods we have added – strip() and check():

```java
import java.io.*;

public class DumbGrep4 {
    public static void main(String argv[]) {
        String word = strip(argv[0]); // this part is new
        String filename = argv[1];
        String optThird = check(argv[0]); // so is this
        String line;
        try {
            FileReader fr = new FileReader(filename);
            BufferedReader br = new BufferedReader(fr);
            while ((line = br.readLine()) != null) {
                if (findIt(line,word,optThird)) {
                    System.out.println(line);
                }
            }
            fr.close();
        } catch (Exception e) {
            System.out.println("Uhoh!");
        }
    }
    . . .
}
```

The strip() method removes the ^ from the search string:

```java
public static String strip(String s) {
    if (s.indexOf("^") == 0) {
        return s.substring(1,s.length());
    } else {
        return s;
    }
}
```

The check() method returns a string that is used to set the optThird variable:

```
public static String check(String s) {
   if (s.indexOf("^") == 0) {
      return "initial";
   } else {
      return "not";
   }
}
```

The findIt method is exactly the same as in DumbGrep3 and so I don't repeat it. There is some redundancy between the two new methods, that we eliminate below.

Let's now revise the program so that it can accommodate searches that specify that the match must occur at the end of the line; for example, as in hat$. There are two main revisions made here. First, we eliminate the redundancy between strip() and check() by combining them into a single method, stripCheck(), that returns an array of strings. Second, we flesh out the findIt() method so that it responds to all four possibilities for the end-of-string markers; for example, hat, ^hat, hat$, and ^hat$. Here is the revised main method:

```
import java.io.*;

public class DumbGrep5 {
   public static void main(String argv[]) {
      // groups the 3 strings together
      String argResults[] = new String[2];
      // invoke the new unified method
      argResults = stripCheck(argv[0]);
      String word = argResults[0];
      String filename = argv[1];
      String optThird = argResults[1];
      String line;
      try {
         FileReader fr = new FileReader(filename);
         BufferedReader br = new BufferedReader(fr);
         while ((line = br.readLine()) != null) {
            if (findIt(line,word,optThird)) {
               System.out.println(line);
            }
         }
         fr.close();
      } catch (Exception e) {
         System.out.println("Uhoh!");
      }
   }
   . . .
```

Here is the combined stripCheck() method:

```
public static String[] stripCheck(String s) {
    String results[] = new String[2];
    // initial and final
    if ((s.indexOf("^") == 0) && (s.indexOf("$") == s.length() - 1)) {
        results[0] = s.substring(1,s.length() - 1);
        results[1] = "if";
    // initial
    } else if (s.indexOf("^") == 0) {
        results[0] = s.substring(1,s.length());
        results[1] = "in";
    // final
    } else if (s.indexOf("$") == s.length() - 1) {
        results[0] = s.substring(0,s.length() - 1);
        results[1] = "nf";
    // any
    } else {
        results[0] = s;
        results[1] = "nn";
    }
    return results;
}
```

I've replaced the initial flag with four new flags – if, in, nf, and nn – to allow for combining the end-of-string markers. Finally, here is the revised findIt() method, which now makes use of these four flags:

```
public static boolean findIt(String theLine,
        String theWord, String third) {
    int where;
    // initial
    if (third.equals("in")) {
        if (theLine.indexOf(theWord) == 0) {
            return true;
        }
    // final
    } else if (third.equals("nf")) {
        where = theLine.indexOf(theWord) + theWord.length();
        if ((where == theLine.length()) &&
                (theLine.indexOf(theWord) > -1)) {
            return true;
        }
    // both
    } else if (third.equals("if")) {
        where = theLine.indexOf(theWord) + theWord.length();
```

```
        if ((where == theLine.length()) &&
            (theLine.indexOf(theWord) == 0)) {
          return true;
        }
    // any
    } else {
        if (theLine.indexOf(theWord) > -1) {
          return true;
        }
    }
    return false;
  }
```

The only new feature here is the use of return. It looks as though findIt()
always ends by returning false, but the final command is only reached if some
previous return statement isn't applied. In other words, within a method, a
return causes the method to stop executing any further statements in that
method.

In later chapters, we will revise the DumbGrep program further. We leave it
as is for now, until we have more resources to develop it with.

5.3   *Summary*

This chapter has introduced the notion of subroutines or methods. These
allow one to separate groups of statements into coherent and reusable chunks.
Methods come in two basic types: ones that simply do something, and ones
that return something, such as an int, String, long, or boolean.

5.4   *Exercises*

1. Revise the DumbGrep program so that it saves its output to a file, the
    name of which is given on the command line.
2. Revise the DumbGrep program so that it handles any errors involving the
    command-line arguments. Make sure you do this by adding separate
    methods.
3. Revise the DumbGrep program so that it takes any number of search
    terms. Each subsequent term must appear to the right of the preceding
    one for the line to match.
4. Revise the DumbGrep program so that all its arguments are given at
    appropriate prompts.

5. Revise the DumbGrep program so it reads in two lines at a time and searches those pairs in sequence. Make sure then that each line is searched twice, once as the first of each two-line unit, and again as the second of each unit. The user should be able to enter search strings that include the line break in the middle of the unit. (This is difficult.)

Note

[1] I've chosen these because they are standard symbols used in other programming languages. See appendix B.

Chapter 6
Objects

This chapter introduces the notion of **object-oriented** (OO) programming. **Inheritance** and **subclassing** are treated by going back through the programs already developed and recasting them in object-oriented terms. Several programs from previous chapters are revised in object-oriented style, and the chapter develops an object-oriented program for tagging words in a sentence, and another for collecting experimental data.

6.1   Classes

So far, we have treated a Java™ program as a sequence of statements grouped by methods and control statements. In a sense, this is true. However, to continue to view Java technology in this way would be to miss out on a lot of the power of the Java language.

The Java programming language is object-oriented like **C++**, rather than procedural like **C**, **Basic**, or **Perl**. What this means is that there is another grouping to Java programs: **objects**.

The template or description of an object is called a **class**. The difference between class and object is roughly analogous to that between generic and specific. When I talk about "apples" in general, I am using the word generically, in reference to general properties of the fruit; for example, that they are round or grow on trees. This is analogous to a class. When I talk about "the apple on my desk", I'm using a specific description, referring to a specific object, that is an instance of the general class of apples.

We have actually seen quite a few objects – or classes – in the programs developed so far. For example, every program is a class. All the readers, writers, and streams in the IO system are classes. In addition, although it isn't as obvious as it should be, Strings are classes.[1]

The basic idea is as follows. First, you must take the particular programming task at hand and re-conceive of it, not as a sequence of steps, but as a network of objects, objects that interact with each other to produce the desired results. These objects will interact with each other via method descriptions associated with each of the objects. Your specific responsibility as programmer will then be to write the class descriptions and methods for the objects that you need.

When your program runs, it will use your static class descriptions to create or *instantiate* the specific objects required. We have, in fact, already seen examples of this instantiation as well. Whenever we used the keyword new with a Java class such as BufferedReader or GZIPInputStream, we were instantiating a class description as a specific object. In this chapter, we will learn how to write our own class descriptions to instantiate as useful objects.

There is one further aspect of classes and objects that we need to understand in advance. Classes include methods, but the methods can be of two types: static or class-level versus **instantiated,** or object-level. Static methods are those that are appropriate to general description. For example, a static method might provide general information about apples; for example, that they grow on trees. An instantiated method, on the other hand, can only be applied to a specific (instantiated) object; for example, where it is, or whether it has been eaten yet.

For example, we have made use of the Integer class when we invoked the static method Integer.parseInt(). On the other hand, an instantiated class is one that has been declared for some specific purpose. For example, we made use of an instantiated method readLine() in the BufferedReader class. The distinction is a subtle, but essential one.

Consider the HelloWorld program from chapter 2, repeated below:

```
public class HelloWorld {
    public static void main(String argv[]) {
        System.out.println("Hello World!");
    }
}
```

This program defines a class HelloWorld. This class is never explicitly instantiated. Instead, it exists in a more abstract sense, and the only way to make use of it is to use any static methods it contains. In this case, HelloWorld contains the static main method.

Let's look more closely at instantiating objects. As mentioned above, an object is instantiated by declaring it with the new codeword.[2] We did this a number of times when we were treating IO in chapter 4. For example, a line such as the following instantiates the class BufferedReader:

```
BufferedReader br = new BufferedReader(fr);
```

The BufferedReader class is defined so that it can be instantiated by taking, for example, a FileReader as an argument. Instantiation of a class that the programmer defines is handled by means of a **constructor** method. The constructor method has the same name as the class itself and has no return type. In effect, the constructor returns an object, an instantiation of the whole class. Here is a revision of the HelloWorld program that instantiates the class, rather than treating it statically:

```
public class HelloWorldOO {
   public HelloWorldOO() {
      System.out.println("Hello World!");
   }
   public static void main(String argv[]) {
      HelloWorldOO hwoo = new HelloWorldOO();
   }
}
```

The program is renamed HelloWorldOO. The first method is the constructor. It has the same name as the program/class, no arguments in this case, and no return type. Constructing or instantiating the class performs the printing. The class also includes the static main. As always, the main method is where the JVM goes first (even though it's listed below the constructor in this example). It has to be declared as static because the class isn't yet instantiated when the main method is run. In this case, the main method simply instantiates the HelloWorldOO class. Thus running a program with java invokes that program's main method. Invoking a class by instantiating it invokes that class's constructor method.

Let's now construct a specific example to follow the apple example above. We will write a class definition Apple. This class includes a static method growWhere() that returns general information about apples – that they grow "on trees". We want to talk about specific apples as well, so there is a constructor that – in this case – spits back the command-line argument that indicates where the specific apple myApple is located:

```
public class Apple {
   public Apple(String loc) {
      System.out.println("My apple is on my " + loc);
   }
   public static String growWhere() {
      return "trees";
   }
```

```
    public static void main(String argv[]) {
        System.out.println("Apples grow on " + growWhere());
        Apple myApple = new Apple(argv[0]);
    }
}
```

Apple is the class and myApple is an object of that class. Notice again that even though the main method is the last method of the class listed, it is still where the JVM goes first. I will follow this system through the book, listing the constructor first, the main last, and other methods in between.

Classes can be invoked by other classes. For example, in a separate file in the same directory, we can write a second program – HWCaller – that simply instantiates HelloWorldOO:

```
public class HWCaller {
    public static void main(String argv[]) {
        HelloWorldOO hwoo = new HelloWorldOO();
    }
}
```

This program defines a class HWCaller that is treated statically. It exists only to hold a static main method which instantiates the HelloWorldOO class. Instantiating the latter invokes its constructor method, printing the familiar message. Invoking HelloWorldOO this way, typing java HWCaller, means that its own main method is not called.

In fact, if we were sure that HelloWorldOO would only be invoked by other classes, and never on its own, we could strip out its own main method as follows:

```
public class HelloWorldOO {
    public HelloWorldOO() {
        System.out.println("Hello World!");
    }
}
```

This new class can still be called by HWCaller. Having multiple class files is a very typical structure for Java programs. A large program can be composed of many separate class files, only one of which contains a main method.

Let's digress for a moment to consider how javac and java handle programs that reside in multiple files. The javac program is run with a filename as an argument. As the compiler goes through the file, it keeps track of any references to other files, and these are compiled as well if necessary. In fact, javac is "smart" enough to detect if there have been changes in the program files since the last time they were compiled. If there have been changes, then these files are recompiled. This is quite convenient, since it typically means that if you have a large program that is distributed in a number of files, you only need to invoke javac once any time you compile the program. The java command is also "smart". You invoke it on a single class file, one that has a main method, and it finds any other class files.[3]

Methods in any class can be formulated as static or instantiated. Returning to the apple example, static methods tell us about apples in general. Instantiated methods, on the other hand, tell us about some specific apple. For example, the following code will *not* work, because the method called by the main method isn't declared as static:

```
public class StaticWRONG {
    // instantiated method
    public void wrong() {
        System.out.println("This won't work!");
    }
    public static void main(String argv[]) {
    // instantiated method call!
        wrong();
    }
}
```

On the other hand, if the class is instantiated, then the method can be called:

```
public class InsMeth {
    // instantiated method
    public void right() {
        System.out.println("This will work!");
    }
    public static void main(String argv[]) {
        // instantiate the object
        InsMeth im = new InsMeth();
        // call the instantiated method via the object
        im.right();
    }
}
```

Notice how a method of an instantiated class is called, by class name and method name, separated by a period. On the other hand, if the method is called internal to the class itself, no class name is needed. Notice too that if no explicit constructor is written, then a no-argument constructor automatically works.

We can do the same thing with the Apple class, which is revised as Apple2 below:

```
public class Apple2 {
   public void foundWhere(String s) {
      System.out.println("myApple is on my " + s);
   }
   public static void growWhere() {
      System.out.println("Apples grow on trees");
   }
   public static void main(String argv[]) {
      growWhere();
      Apple2 myApple = new Apple2();
      myApple.foundWhere(argv[0]);
   }
}
```

The growWhere() method is static and can be called before myApple is instantiated. The foundWhere() method is instantiated and can only be called with respect to a specific Apple2 object.[4]

Variables can also be static or instantiated if they are declared directly in the class. Declaring a variable directly in the class makes it available to all methods of that class:

```
public class Vbloo1 {
   int n;
   static int m = 0;
   public Vbloo1(String k) {
      n = Integer.parseInt(k);
      m++;
   }
   public static void main(String argv[]) {
      Vbloo1 vb1 = new Vbloo1(argv[0]);
      Vbloo1 vb2 = new Vbloo1(argv[1]);
      System.out.println("vb1.n: " + vb1.n);
      System.out.println("vb2.n: " + vb2.n);
      System.out.println("Vbloo1.m: " + Vbloo1.m);
   }
}
```

The class Vbloo1 defines two integer variables, one instantiated and the other static. The constructor takes a string argument, converts it to an integer and assigns it to the first (instantiated) integer. It then adds one to the second (static) integer variable. The main method instantiates the class twice with its two command-line arguments. It then prints out the values of n associated with each instantiation and the value of m associated with the class.

Thus the instantiations have access to the instantiated variables of each object. The static variable is available to both, as vb1.m or vb2.m, but is also available from the uninstantiated class as Vbloo1.m. Notice how the static variable – being independent of the instantiations – thus keeps track of the number of instantiations, incrementing each time the constructor method is called. This is a powerful device, as we will see. Notice how the constructor refers to each variable directly without a preceding class name. This is the general case for variables defined within a class directly; they are available to all methods of that class.

This allows for two solutions to passing the value of a variable between methods. One possibility is to declare the variable within a method and pass its value as arguments to other methods. Another possibility is to declare the variable directly in the class, so that it need not be made an argument to other methods. These two strategies are exemplified below. The first program Vbloo2 declares the variable n in the constructor and then passes n to printIt() as an explicit argument. Since the variable is declared *within* a method, it is not available outside that method (the constructor method here) unless it is explicitly passed:

```
public class Vbloo2 {
    public Vbloo2(String k) {
        int n = Integer.parseInt(k);
        printIt(n);
    }
    public void printIt(int i) {
        System.out.println("n = " + i);
    }
    public static void main(String argv[]) {
        Vbloo2 vb1 = new Vbloo2(argv[0]);
    }
}
```

The second program Vbloo3 declares the variable n directly in the class. Both the constructor and printIt() can refer to the variable n directly, and there is no need to pass it as an explicit argument to printIt():

```
public class Vbloo3 {
    int n;
    public Vbloo3(String k) {
        n = Integer.parseInt(k);
        printIt();
    }
    public void printIt() {
        System.out.println("n = " + n);
    }
    public static void main(String argv[]) {
        Vbloo3 vb1 = new Vbloo3(argv[0]);
    }
}
```

This difference between the behavior of the variables can also be seen in the actual letters we use. In Vbloo3, we *must* use the same variable name n throughout. In Vbloo2, we can use a different name in each method.

6.2 *Searching Text with Objects*

Let's now revise our DumbGrep program so that it is more in line with object-oriented programming style. To do this, we must first rethink the tasks of the program in terms of objects. There are an infinite number of ways to do this, so I'll just go with what seems most natural. First, there should be some sort of overarching class: GrepOO. There should be something to read the input file: MyReader, something to parse the arguments: ArgParser, and finally something to search: Searcher. I go through each of these in turn. The first class is the GrepOO class:

```
public class GrepOO {
    public GrepOO(String[] a) {
        ArgParser ap = new ArgParser(a);
        MyReader mr = new MyReader(ap);
    }
    public static void main(String argv[]) {
        GrepOO g = new GrepOO(argv);
    }
}
```

This class is just a frame for calling the more substantive classes. There is only a constructor and the main method. The main method simply declares the GrepOO class. This calls the constructor. The constructor declares an ArgParser, which is then used to declare the MyReader class.

Let's look at the ArgParser class next:

```
public class ArgParser {
    // class-level search string variable
    String pat;
    String filename;
    String edge;
    // constructor
    public ArgParser(String[] a) {
        pat = a[0];
        filename = a[1];
        stripCheck();
    }
    // no changes to this method
    void stripCheck() {
```

```
    if ((pat.indexOf("^") == 0) &&
        (pat.indexOf("$") == pat.length() - 1)) {
      pat = pat.substring(1,pat.length() - 1);
      edge = "if";
    } else if (pat.indexOf("^") == 0) {
      pat = pat.substring(1,pat.length());
      edge = "in";
    } else if (pat.indexOf("$") == pat.length() - 1) {
      pat = pat.substring(0,pat.length() - 1);
      edge = "nf";
    } else {
      edge = "nn";
    }
  }
  // accessor methods
  public String getPat() {
    return pat;
  }
  public String getFilename() {
    return filename;
  }
  public String getEdge() {
    return edge;
  }
}
```

The guts of the ArgParser class is the old stripCheck() method (on page 51 above). What this class does is parse the command-line arguments to GrepOO and assign them to individual variables. In addition, this class provides a set of methods: getPat(), getFilename(), and getEdge(). These are called **accessor** methods. What they allow us to do is to *hide* the details of how the arguments are passed to the next class, MyReader. This is a standard aspect of object-oriented programming.

Here is MyReader:

```
import java.io.*;

public class MyReader {
  String pattern;
  String filename;
  String edge;
  // constructor sets variables with accessor methods
  public MyReader(ArgParser ap) {
    filename = ap.getFilename();
    pattern = ap.getPat();
```

```
         edge = ap.getEdge();
         doFileIO();
   }
   void doFileIO() {
      // declares a Searcher object
      Searcher search;
      String line;
      try {
         FileReader fr = new FileReader(filename);
         BufferedReader br = new BufferedReader(fr);
         while ((line = br.readLine()) != null) {
            search = new Searcher(line,pattern,edge);
         }
         fr.close();
      } catch (Exception e) {
         e.printStackTrace();
      }
   }
}
```

The MyReader class does three things. First, in its constructor, it takes the arguments massaged by ArgParser and assigns them to new variables. Notice how this is all shielded from the GrepOO frame class. Second, it does all the old file IO. Finally, it uses the new variable assignments to instantiate a new class: Searcher. Notice that this new class is called somewhat differently from the others. In the other cases, only a single instance of each class was created. Here, though the class is declared only once, it is reinstantiated for each line of the file. This is because the critical work of the Searcher class is done by its constructor. Finally, notice how doFileIO() handles exceptions with a call to printStackTrace(). This command prints out a detailed listing of the nature and source of the exception.

Finally, we have the Searcher class:

```
public class Searcher {
   public Searcher(String l, String p, String e) {
      int where;
      if (e.equals("in")) {
         if (l.indexOf(p) == 0) {
            System.out.println(l);
         }
      } else if (e.equals("nf")) {
         where = l.indexOf(p) + p.length();
         if ((where == l.length()) && (l.indexOf(p) > -1)) {
            System.out.println(l);
         }
```

```
        } else if (e.equals("if")) {
          where = l.indexOf(p) + p.length();
          if ((where == l.length()) && (l.indexOf(p) == 0)) {
            System.out.println(l);
          }
        } else {
          if (l.indexOf(p) > -1) {
            System.out.println(l);
          }
        }
      }
    }
  }
```

The guts of the Searcher class is its constructor which, in turn, is built on the old findIt() method. Constructing the Searcher performs the actual search.

It's not clear that the mechanisms of OO programming are any more efficient, given what we have done with them so far. They do, however, offer a rather different way of viewing programming tasks, one that may be more or less intuitive for different programmers. With larger projects, there are some very clear advantages to an OO style, and this is presented in the next section.

6.3   *Inheritance*

Object-oriented programming offers another feature: **inheritance**. A class can be defined to *extend* another already defined class. What this means is that the new daughter class takes on any features of the defining class that it does not explicitly supercede. To return to the apple example earlier in the chapter, we might define some class Fruit that defines methods appopriate to fruits in general. We could then define a class Apple that inherits from the Fruit class, but that adds specific methods appropriate to apples.

Consider the following examples. The class Parent1 contains a single method printSomething():

```
public class Parent1 {
  public void printSomething(String s) {
    System.out.println(s);
  }
}
```

The class Daughter1 is defined to extend the Parent1 class; it defines no methods of its own:

```
public class Daughter1 extends Parent1 {
   public static void main(String argv[]) {
      Daughter1 d = new Daughter1();
      d.printSomething("an inherited method");
   }
}
```

Nonetheless, the method printSomething() is available to Daughter1; it is *inherited* from Parent1.

Class variables can also be inherited. The class Daughter2 inherits from Parent2. The latter defines a class variable that the former can access:

```
public class Parent2 {
   int n;
   public Parent2() {
      n = 2;
   }
}
```

```
public class Daughter2 extends Parent2 {
   public static void main(String argv[]) {
      Daughter2 d = new Daughter2();
      System.out.println("d.n = " + d.n);
   }
}
```

The inheriting class can override inherited features simply by declaring or defining them itself. The Daughter3 class inherits from Parent2, but re-defines n:

```
public class Daughter3 extends Parent2 {
   int n;
   public Daughter3() {
      n = 5;
   }
   public static void main(String argv[]) {
      Daughter3 d = new Daughter3();
      System.out.println("d.n = " + d.n);
   }
}
```

This is a very powerful device, but there are limits. A class can only extend *one* class directly. It is not possible to put two or more class names after the extends term. On the other hand, inheritance is transitive. A class can inherit variables and methods from far up its inheritance chain.

Inheritance is a very useful device if one has closely related objects. Rather than writing code for objects that repeats the same methods and variables again and again, a set of inheritance relations can be set up so that related classes have access to the same methods and variables.

6.4   *Interactive Tagging*

Various linguistic problems lend themselves nicely to a treatment in terms of inheritance. In this section, we develop a program that collects information about words in a sentence. The program takes advantage of inheritance to define different word classes. The general program is a little unrealistic as a means of collecting such data, but the goal here is to illustrate how inheritance works and how it is relevant for linguistic tasks.

The basic task is as follows. The program is invoked with a string of words on the command line. The program then collects appropriate information on each word. This information includes general information appropriate to any word of English, along with specific information appropriate to specific parts of speech. For example, any word of English might be borrowed from another language, but only verbs can be transitive. Here is a sample interaction with the program, called Sentence (text typed by the user is in bold face):

```
> java Sentence Joe has a sombrero
"Joe": noun(n), verb(v), adjective(a), other(o): n
word: Joe, pos: n
Is the word borrowed? (y/n): n
Is the noun a proper noun? (y/n): y
"has": noun(n), verb(v), adjective(a), other(o): v
word: has, pos: v
Is the word borrowed? (y/n): n
Is the verb transitive? (y/n): y
"a": noun(n), verb(v), adjective(a), other(o): o
word: a, pos: o
Is the word borrowed? (y/n): n
"sombrero": noun(n), verb(v), adjective(a), other(o): n
word: sombrero, pos: n
Is the word borrowed? (y/n): y
Is the noun a proper noun? (y/n): n
```

The program could make use of this sort of information in any number of ways but, for pedagogical purposes, it's set up here to immediately display a summary of the information collected:

```
Joe
part of speech: noun
borrowed: no
proper noun: yes
has
part of speech: verb
borrowed: no
transitive: yes
a
part of speech: other
borrowed: no
sombrero
part of speech: noun
borrowed: yes
proper noun: no
```

Let's now look at the code. First, there is the main class Sentence. This class has a main method, a constructor, and three other methods: query(), makeWord(), and getInfo(). This class holds an array of words, constructed from its command-line arguments. The query() and makeWord() methods are used to construct the array, and the getInfo() method returns the information stored in the array.

When invoked as in the above example, the JVM goes first to the main method. That, in turn, passes the command-line arguments to the constructor for the Sentence class. Once all the information about the words has been collected, via the methods and objects invoked by the constructor, the main method calls the getInfo() method to display the results.

Let's now look at the class variables for Sentence. First, there is an array of objects that are defined as being of the class Word. This array will hold the information on each word in the command line. Second, there is a string variable POS which is defined as static and final. The static part means that it's available at the class level. The final designation means that the value of this variable cannot be changed, that it is a **constant**. If you never change the value of some variable, then you should declare it as static and final. For technical reasons, this allows the program to run more quickly. It is customary to capitalize the names of constants. This particular constant is used by the constructor to check whether the user answers the part-of-speech question appropriately.

The class constructor itself is rather straightforward; it invokes the query() method, going through the command-line arguments one by one collecting part-of-speech information. It uses that information as arguments to the makeWord() method. Note the embedded while-loop. This is used to force the user to give an appropriate response when asked for part-of-speech.

The makeWord() method is also straightforward. It takes three arguments: the word, its part-of-speech, and an index that represents the position in the sentence that the word occupies. The body of the method is an if-structure that adds the appropriate word class to the array.

The code for Sentence reveals five other Java classes in this program: Word, Noun, Adjective, Verb, and Other. The fact that the sentence array is defined over Word objects, but makeWord() adds specific word types, tells us something else as well. It must be the case that Noun, Verb, Adjective, and Other are subclasses of Word, that they inherit from Word. Thus a Noun can be added to the Word array sentence, because Noun is a kind of Word.

Here is the Sentence class:

```java
import java.io.*;

public class Sentence {
    Word[] sentence;
    static final String POS = "nvao";
    public Sentence(String[] words) {
        sentence = new Word[words.length];
        query(words);
    }
    private void query(String[] s) {
        String line;
        try {
            InputStreamReader isr = new InputStreamReader(System.in);
            BufferedReader br = new BufferedReader(isr);
            for (int i = 0; i < sentence.length; i++) {
                line = "";
                while ((POS.indexOf(line) < 0) || (line.length() != 1)) {
                    System.out.print("\"" + s[i] + "\": noun(n), " +
                        "verb(v), adjective(a), other(o): ");
                    line = br.readLine();
                }
                makeWord(s[i],line,i);
            }
            br.close();
        } catch (Exception e) {
            e.printStackTrace();
        }
    }
    private void makeWord(String word, String pos, int index) {
        System.out.println("word: " + word + ", pos: " + pos);
        if (pos.equals("n")) {
            sentence[index] = new Noun(word);
        } else if (pos.equals("v")) {
```

```
              sentence[index] = new Verb(word);
          } else if (pos.equals("a")) {
              sentence[index] = new Adjective(word);
          } else {
              sentence[index] = new Other(word);
          }
      }
      public String getInfo() {
          String info = "";
          for (int i = 0; i < sentence.length; i++) {
              info = info + sentence[i].getWord() +
                  "\n" + sentence[i].getInfo();
          }
          return info;
      }
      public static void main(String argv[]) {
          Sentence s = new Sentence(argv);
          System.out.println(s.getInfo());
      }
  }
```

The Word class is defined as abstract. This means that we do not expect to ever instantiate it directly. This is true in the Sentence program: we never try to invoke Word directly, say with new. Making Word an abstract class means that the only work it does will be by the classes that *extend* it; for example, Noun, Verb, Adjective, and Other.

There are *two* constructors for Word, one with one argument, and one with two. The logic here is that to create a new Word, you need to say what the word is. If that's all it's told, then the user will be prompted to supply whether or not it's borrowed. Alternatively, the class can be constructed from two arguments, the second of which indicates whether the word is borrowed. In that case, of course, there is no need to ask the user for that information. There are class-level variables for the word, part-of-speech, and whether it's borrowed. These are defined as private and are thus not available outside of the class. There are accessor methods for all three.

There are some strange things here too. First, notice that the Word class does not set the pos variable. Second, there is a final method getInfo() that is defined as abstract. It has no method body and the declaration ends with a semicolon. If a class contains such a method, the class itself must be defined as abstract (as Word is). What this means is that any class that extends Word is *required* to provide a getInfo() method.

The logic of the program is that the getInfo() method of Sentence uses the getInfo() method of each Word subclass to collect information about each word in the sentence:

```
import java.io.*;

public abstract class Word {
    private String word, pos;
    private boolean borrowed;
    public Word(String s) {
        word = s;
        setBorrowed();
    }
    public Word(String s, boolean b) {
        word = s;
        borrowed = b;
    }
    private void setBorrowed() {
        System.out.print("Is the word borrowed? (y/n): ");
        try {
            InputStreamReader isr = new InputStreamReader(System.in);
            BufferedReader br = new BufferedReader(isr);
            String answer = br.readLine();
            if (answer.equals("y")) {
                borrowed = true;
            } else {
                borrowed = false;
            }
        } catch (Exception e) {
            e.printStackTrace();
        }
    }
    public boolean getBorrowed() {return borrowed; }
    public String getWord() {return word; }
    public void setPos(String s) {pos = s; }
    public String getPos() {return pos; }
    abstract String getInfo();
}
```

Let's now consider the Noun class. First, as expected, it extends the Word class, and – as expected again – defines a getInfo() method. This class inherits all the class-level variables and methods of the Word class. In addition, it defines two constructors, a private boolean variable proper and an accessor method for that variable.

The first constructor invokes Noun with only the word string. In that case, Noun calls the constructor of its superclass Word with the method super(). That call to the Word constructor invokes the setBorrowed() method of Word, querying the user for whether this noun is borrowed. Next, the Noun constructor continues by invoking the setPos() method. Noun does not have such a method itself, but inherits it from Word. Finally, the constructor invokes the setProper() method of Noun to ask the user about whether the noun is a proper noun.

The second constructor takes three arguments, allowing a Noun object to be instantiated without user interaction.

The Noun class thus takes advantage of several methods of the Word class – setPos() and setBorrowed():

```java
import java.io.*;

public class Noun extends Word {
    private boolean proper;
    public Noun(String s) {
        super(s);
        setPos("noun");
        setProper();
    }
    public Noun(String s, boolean b, boolean p) {
        super(s,b);
        setPos("noun");
        proper = p;
    }
    private void setProper() {
        System.out.print("Is the noun a proper noun? (y/n): ");
        try {
            InputStreamReader isr = new InputStreamReader(System.in);
            BufferedReader br = new BufferedReader(isr);
            String answer = br.readLine();
            if (answer.equals("y")) {
                proper = true;
            } else {
                proper = false;
            }
        } catch (Exception e) {
            e.printStackTrace();
        }
    }
    public boolean getProper() {return proper; }
    public String getInfo() {
        String theInfo = "part of speech: " + getPos() + "\n";
        theInfo = theInfo + "borrowed: ";
        if (getBorrowed()) {
            theInfo = theInfo + "yes\n";
        } else {
            theInfo = theInfo + "no\n";
        }
```

```
        theInfo = theInfo + "proper noun: ";
        if (getProper()) {
           theInfo = theInfo + "yes\n";
        } else {
           theInfo = theInfo + "no\n";
        }
        return theInfo;
    }
}
```

The Verb class is parallel. It has essentially the same structure as the Noun class, except that it defines methods and variables that deal with whether the verb is transitive. Like the Noun class, Verb makes use of setBorrowed() and setPos() from Word. This use of inherited methods is the real power of object subclassing and inheritance:

```
import java.io.*;

public class Verb extends Word {
    private boolean transitive;
    public Verb(String s) {
        super(s);
        setPos("verb");
        setTransitive();
    }
    public Verb(String s, boolean b, boolean t) {
        super(s,b);
        setPos("verb");
        transitive = t;
    }
    private void setTransitive() {
        System.out.print("Is the verb transitive? (y/n): ");
        try {
           InputStreamReader isr = new InputStreamReader(System.in);
           BufferedReader br = new BufferedReader(isr);
           String answer = br.readLine();
           if (answer.equals("y")) {
              transitive = true;
           } else {
              transitive = false;
           }
        } catch (Exception e) {
           e.printStackTrace();
        }
    }
```

```
      public boolean getTransitive() {return transitive; }
      public String getInfo() {
         String theInfo = "part of speech: " + getPos() + "\n";
         theInfo = theInfo + "borrowed: ";
         if (getBorrowed()) {
            theInfo = theInfo + "yes\n";
         } else {
            theInfo = theInfo + "no\n";
         }
         theInfo = theInfo + "transitive: ";
         if (getTransitive()) {
            theInfo = theInfo + "yes\n";
         } else {
            theInfo = theInfo + "no\n";
         }
         return theInfo;
      }
   }
```

Finally, here are the Adjective and Other classes. They don't define additional methods, but it would be a trivial matter to introduce appropriate ones (this is left as an exercise):

```
public class Adjective extends Word {
   public Adjective(String s) {
      super(s);
      setPos("adjective");
   }
   public Adjective(String s, boolean b) {
      super(s,b);
      setPos("adjective");
   }
   public String getInfo() {
      String theInfo = "part of speech: " + getPos() + "\n";
      theInfo = theInfo + "borrowed: ";
      if (getBorrowed()) {
         theInfo = theInfo + "yes\n";
      } else {
         theInfo = theInfo + "no\n";
      }
      return theInfo;
   }
}

public class Other extends Word {
   public Other(String s) {
```

```
            super(s);
            setPos("other");
        }
        public Other(String s, boolean b) {
            super(s,b);
            setPos("other");
        }
        public String getInfo() {
            String theInfo = "part of speech: " + getPos() + "\n";
            theInfo = theInfo + "borrowed: ";
            if (getBorrowed()) {
                theInfo = theInfo + "yes\n";
            } else {
                theInfo = theInfo + "no\n";
            }
            return theInfo;
        }
    }
```

6.5   *Collecting Experimental Data*

In this section, we develop a program for collecting experimental data. The program is written in object-oriented style and makes use of inheritance. The program is preliminary and will be revised significantly in subsequent chapters.

Let's start with a very simple task. You, as experimenter, wish to collect subjects' judgments about a set of sentences. You want to know which sentences your subjects think sound fine, and which they think sound bad. You want to run this task on a group of subjects, and then analyze the results statistically.

Let's now think about the task in more concrete terms. Let's assume that the materials are in a text file. This file can be read by the experiment program – let's call it Exp. The program will present the items one by one and store the responses. It will then write the items and their responses to a second file.

Here is the framework for the Exp program:

```
public class Exp {
    public Exp(String f, String s) {
        Materials m = new Materials(f);
        YesNoQuery q = new YesNoQuery(m,s);
    }
    public static void main(String argv[]) {
        if (argv.length != 2) {
            System.out.println("Enter a filename and subject code");
```

```
        } else {
            Exp e = new Exp(argv[0],argv[1]);
        }
    }
}
```

First, there is the main method. It checks that there are two command-line arguments and passes them to the constructor for the Exp class. The Exp class constructor creates two other objects: Materials and YesNoQuery. The Materials class reads the items in from the materials file, while the YesNoQuery class presents the items and collects the responses.

I assume that the materials come in a specific format. Specifically, the file is a text file, each item is given on a separate line, and the number of items is given on the first line. For example:

```
4
John loves Mary.
Mary loves John.
loves Mary John.
John Mary loves.
```

Let's now look at the Materials class. Several variables are defined at the class level: filename for the name of the materials file, and items[] for the experimental items. The constructor assigns a value to filename and invokes the core method of this class – doIO():

```
import java.io.*;

public class Materials {
    String filename;
    String items[];
    public Materials(String f) {
        filename = f;
        doIO();
    }
    . . .
```

The doIO() method reads the materials from the materials file. There are a couple of interesting things about it. First, it is declared as private. This means that the method cannot be called from outside the Materials class. As a rule of thumb, declaring methods and variables as private is helpful as a way of forcing one to think about the ways the classes of your program should be interacting. A second thing to note about doIO() is the way br.readLine() is called outside the while structure. This shouldn't be surprising, but this is, in fact, the first time we have done this. Notice how we use the integer read from the materials file to set the size of the items[] array.[5] Finally, as each line is read from the file, it is copied to the array items:

```
private void doIO() {
    String line;
    int i = 0;
    try {
        FileReader fr = new FileReader(filename);
        BufferedReader br = new BufferedReader(fr);
        int n = Integer.parseInt(br.readLine());
        items = new String[n];
        while ((line = br.readLine()) != null) {
            items[i++] = line;
        }
        fr.close();
    } catch (Exception e) {
        e.printStackTrace();
    }
}
```

Finally, there is an accessor method getItems() for returning the experimental items:

```
public String[] getItems() {
    return items;
}
```

Let's now look at the YesNoQuery class. What we want is a set of methods for displaying the experimental materials and then recording the responses. In the experiment at hand, all we really want is to collect a yes–no response, but we might want our Exp program to be able to deal with more complex experiments. For example, we might want to collect reaction times or display images, or allow for a wider range of responses.

To allow for this, we'll define an abstract class Query. This sets up the general template for an experiment, but must be subclassed or extended by another class to run any particular type of experiment. Let's look at the details. The class is defined as abstract. This means that javac will display an error if an attempt is made to instantiate Query directly. The class defines several class-level variables. The preamble is for storing the text that is displayed before the experimental item. The finish variable stores the text after the item. The subject, filename, items[], and results[] variables are self-explanatory.

The constructor for this class assigns values to items[] and subject, and initializes the other variables. It then calls three methods that we will go through in turn:

```
import java.io.*;

public abstract class Query {
    String preamble, finish, subject, filename;
    String[] items;
    String[] results;
    public Query(Materials m, String s) {
        items = m.getItems();
        subject = s;
        results = new String[items.length];
        preamble = "";
        finish = "";
        filename = "";
        makeBits();
        display();
        saveResults();
    }
    . . .
```

The makeBits() method is defined as abstract. In terms of syntax, this means that there is no method body, only a semicolon (which is easily forgotten and a common source of errors). The abstract designation for the method means that any class extending the Query class *must* define the makeBits() method. If it does not, javac will produce an error.

The logic of the Query class is that makeBits() is where the preamble and finish variables are defined. In addition, filename, the name of the results file, is also defined here:

```
abstract void makeBits();
```

The next method is the display() method. This method uses the variables defined by makeBits() to display the experimental items. It collects the responses by using prompt input:

```
private void display() {
    try {
        InputStreamReader isr;
        isr = new InputStreamReader(System.in);
        BufferedReader br;
        br = new BufferedReader(isr);
        for (int i = 0; i < items.length; i++) {
            System.out.println();
            System.out.println(preamble);
            System.out.println(items[i]);
            System.out.print(finish);
```

```
            System.out.flush();
            results[i] = br.readLine();
        }
        br.close();
    } catch (Exception e) {
        System.out.println("Something went wrong. Please inform" +
            " the experimentor");
    }
}
```

Finally, we have the saveResults() method. This method saves the results to a file. There are three things to notice. First, notice that FileWriter is invoked with an extra true argument. When invoked like this, FileWriter opens a file and *appends* data, as opposed to wiping out anything already there. This allows us to run the experiment repeatedly and add new results to an existing file. Second, the results are written in a particular format. The idea is that we want our statistical software to be able to manipulate the results later. I assume that tab-delimited columns will be something that that software can make sense of. Finally, notice that we need to use a special character to represent a tab in a print statement – \t:

```
private void saveResults() {
    try {
        FileWriter fr = new FileWriter(filename,true);
        BufferedWriter br = new BufferedWriter(fr);
        PrintWriter pw = new PrintWriter(br);
        for (int i = 0; i < results.length; i++) {
            pw.println(subject + "\t" + items[i] +
                "\t" + results[i]);
        }
        pw.flush();
        fr.close();
    } catch (Exception e) {
        System.out.println("Error writing to results file.");
    }
}
```

Let's now look at the YesNoQuery class:

```
public class YesNoQuery extends Query {
    public YesNoQuery(Materials m, String s) {
        super(m,s);
    }
    void makeBits() {
        preamble = "Is this sentence grammatical?";
```

```
        finish = "yes(y) or no(n): ";
        filename = "exptest.txt";
    }
}
```

First, notice the constructor; it includes the statement super(m,s). This statement invokes the constructor of the parent class Query. Other than this, the YesNoQuery class simply assigns values to the relevant variables in makeBits().[6]

Imagine we run Exp twice with the following command lines:

```
java Exp exp.txt s1
java Exp exp.txt s2
```

Assuming that our subjects provide the expected judgments, this produces the following for the exptest.txt file:

```
s1 John loves Mary. y
s1 Mary loves John. y
s1 loves Mary John. n
s1 John Mary loves. n
s2 John loves Mary. y
s2 Mary loves John. y
s2 loves Mary John. n
s2 John Mary loves. n
```

6.6 *Summary*

This chapter has introduced the huge topic of object-oriented programming in the Java language. The basic idea is that programs are viewed as a network of interacting things, rather than as a sequence of steps.

Objects allow us to limit the ways data can be manipulated, by providing each object with specific methods whereby the data of that object (the contents of its various class-level variables) can be accessed. In addition, objects allow for inheritance which, in larger programming projects, can allow for greater economy. Objects were exemplified in several larger programs: GrepOO, Sentence, and Exp.

6.7 *Exercises*

1. Write a new IO class that will take a file as an argument and includes a method that returns *two* lines at a time.

2. Revise GrepOO so that it can deal with disjunction. For example, if given a search string h[ao]t, a match is detected with either "hat" or "hot" (but not "hit").
3. Revise the Adjective and Other classes to provide appropriate methods for those parts-of-speech.
4. Write some additional subclasses of Other that inherit from Other (and indirectly from Word).
5. Revise the Exp program so that it checks the responses the subject gives.
6. Write a new class RTQuery, extending Query, that allows you to collect reaction times.

Notes

[1] On the other hand, long and int are not classes.

[2] There are some very unfortunate syntactic properties to the Java language that confuse things. Arrays are also initialized with the keyword new, but are not objects *per se*. Strings don't have to be initialized with new, but are objects. Go figure.

[3] If these files are in the current directory, javac and java will find them. If they are not, javac and java can find them only if the **classpath** option is set to include the location of the files. This can be done on the command line with the -classpath flag, or by setting the CLASSPATH variable globally. How you do the latter depends on your specific operating system.

[4] Here the static method doesn't take an argument, but this is not an essential part of the distinction. For example, Integer.parseInt() is a static method too, but it can take an argument.

[5] We'll see later that there is a more elegant way to do this with the Vector class.

[6] Other classes might extend Query more dramatically, as we'll see later.

Chapter 7
Text Manipulation

This chapter introduces the Java™ **API** (**Application Programming Interface**), the set of classes that come in any Java implementation. These classes enable the programmer to handle many tasks simply by calling an existing class or method, as opposed to writing it yourself from scratch.

This chapter also introduces some of the more useful utilities for manipulating text in depth. These allow for detailed examination and manipulation of text. The chapter uses these utilities to enhance the GrepOO program introduced earlier. In addition, it's shown how to construct a concordance using the same utilities.

7.1   The Java API

We have seen that some commands are only available with a long prefix or with an explicit import statement. For example, the BufferedReader class has to be invoked either as java.io.BufferedReader, or with an import statement; that is, import java.io.*;.

This is because Java technology is broken up into **packages**, groups of related classes and methods. The core is in a package called java.lang, and classes and methods from this package are always available, without any explicit import statement. There are a number of other packages that provide a huge amount of functionality. There's no way we can treat them all here, and most programmers will only be familiar with only the most essential classes for their own projects. However, I'll go through the basic packages here briefly[1] (there are others):

java.applet   This package provides support for **applets**, Java programs that run over the web in a client browser.

java.awt   This and its subpackages provide support for graphics and **graphical user interfaces.**

java.beans   This provides classes and methods for interacting with other "component" software; for example, **OpenDoc**, Microsoft **OLE/ActiveX.**

java.io   This provides support for IO.

java.math   This package includes extended mathematics.

java.net   This is for networking.

java.rmi   This allows for distributed computing, a single Java program running on several different computers at the same time.

java.security   This is for access control, digital certificates, and so on.

java.sql   This package provides classes and methods for dealing with databases.

java.text   Despite the suggestive name, this package is actually for internationalization, writing software that runs appropriately for the language of the user.

java.util   This is an extremely useful set of utilities. It allows for text manipulation, richer data structures, compression, and so on.

java.accessibility   Assistive technology.[2]

javax.swing   This allows for very portable graphics.[3]

A number of these are treated in more depth in subsequent chapters. User interfaces are treated in chapter 8. Graphics are presented in chapter 9. Applets are presented in chapter 10, and javax.swing is discussed in appendix A. The remainder of this chapter deals with some important classes from the java.util package.

7.2   *Chunking and the* StringTokenizer *Class*

One of the most useful classes of the java.util package is the StringTokenizer class. This class provides methods for parsing a string into word-sized chunks. Let's show how it works with an example. This program takes a file (as an argument on the command line) and prints out its contents word by word:

```
import java.io.*;
import java.util.*;

public class Util1 {
    public static void main(String argv[]) {
        String line, word;
        StringTokenizer st;
        try {
```

```
        FileReader fr = new FileReader(argv[0]);
        BufferedReader br = new BufferedReader(fr);
        while ((line = br.readLine()) != null) {
            st = new StringTokenizer(line);
            while (st.hasMoreTokens()) {
                word = st.nextToken();
                System.out.println(word);
            }
        }
        br.close();
    } catch (Exception e) {
        e.printStackTrace();
    }
  }
}
```

The code for Util1 begins with two import statements. The first is for the file IO, and the second is for the StringTokenizer class. The program includes the usual readers for file IO, and some added bits for the StringTokenizer class. First, the class is declared at the outset. It is initialized within the while-loop; each time a line is read, a new StringTokenizer is instantiated. These instances are used in the nested while-loop. The StringTokenizer provides for word **tokens** and the nested while-loop allows for those tokens to be peeled off and printed.

The tokens provided by StringTokenizer – when invoked with only the string as an argument – are any string of characters separated by the following: the space character, the tab character, the new line character, the carriage-return character, and the form-feed character. However, StringTokenizer can be invoked with an optional second argument that specifies what characters to take as delimiters. For example, if the code above is revised so that st is initialized as follows, then only space is taken as a delimiter:

```
st = new StringTokenizer(line," ");
```

Another option provided by the StringTokenizer class is to return the delimiters. This is done by appending a true as the third argument to the instantiation. For example:

```
st = new StringTokenizer(line," ", true);
```

The default behavior is not to return the delimiters.

We will see that the StringTokenizer class is an extremely useful one for any type of parsing task.

7.3   Data Structures

Let's now turn to some of the data structures that are useful for text processing, but that we haven't had a chance to treat yet.

7.3.1   StringBuffer

The first of these is the StringBuffer class, which is actually part of the java.lang package.[4] This differs minimally from the String class that we have been using extensively. The key difference is that the StringBuffer class can be manipulated internally; substrings can be plucked out of it or inserted into it.

As an example of its use, we'll write a little program that plays **Pig Latin** with a word given as command-line input. Recall that the game is played by moving the initial consonants of a word to the right and adding the vowel "ay"; for example, "string" becomes "ingstray", and so on. I call the program PigLatin and it includes several methods. First, there are several class-level variables and a constructor. The class-level variables store the input form and the output form:

```
public class PigLatin {
   String input,result;
   public PigLatin(String s) {
      input = s;
      makeRes();
   }
   . . .
```

There is a main method which calls the constructor with a command-line argument. In addition, the output form is produced by printing the results of a call to getResult():

```
public static void main(String argv[]) {
   PigLatin pl = new PigLatin(argv[0]);
   System.out.println(pl.getResult());
}
```

The getResult() method is trivial; it simply returns the class-level variable result:

```
public String getResult() {
   return result;
}
```

The more interesting methods are makeRes() and consonant(). The logic of the makeRes() method is that it will strip off segments from the left of the input as long as they are consonants. The consonant() method provides a test for whether a character is a consonant. The only real interest of the consonant() method is that it makes use of a new data type – char, for character:[5]

```
private boolean consonant(char c) {
    String consonants = "bcdfghjklmnpqrstvwxyz";
    if (consonants.indexOf(c) > -1) {
        return true;
    } else {
        return false;
    }
}
```

Let's now turn to the makeRes() method:

```
private void makeRes() {
    StringBuffer sb = new StringBuffer(input);
    StringBuffer prefix = new StringBuffer("");
    while (consonant(sb.charAt(0))) {
        prefix.append(sb.charAt(0));
        sb.deleteCharAt(0);
    }
    if (prefix.length() == 0) {
        prefix.append("y");
    }
    sb.append(prefix.toString());
    sb.append("ay");
    result = sb.toString();
}
```

The makeRes() method builds a StringBuffer from the class-level input variable. It builds a second method-internal variable called prefix, which will be where the consonants to be moved to the right end of the word are stored. The method then loops on the first consonant of sb. If it is a consonant, then it is appended to prefix and deleted from sb.[6] Eventually, the program will reach a vowel and exit the while-loop. In the particular version of the game represented here, if there is no consonant, then "y" is appended instead. The next if structure handles this. Next, prefix and "ay" are appended on the end of sb and the results are put in the string variable result.

There are several new methods here that are specific to StringBuffer. Notice in particular that the StringBuffer must be converted to a string before it can be assigned to result. The StringBuffer class is a very convenient one, but most of its functionality can actually be gotten with clever use of string variables.

StringBuffer.deleteCharAt() workaround
The PigLatin program of the previous section makes use of the deleteCharAt() method of the StringBuffer class. This method was only introduced in Java 1.2, and is therefore currently unavailable on Macs or in Applets.[7] The following program provides a workaround. The relevant line of PigLatin should be replaced with the following:

```
sb = FixIt1.deleteCharAt(sb,0);
```

The FixIt1 class defines two static methods that will do the work of the built-in deleteCharAt() method. Here's the code:

```
public class FixIt1 {
    public static String deleteCharAt(String s, int i) {
        String suffix = s.substring(i+1);
        String prefix = s.substring(0,i);
        s = prefix + suffix;
        return s;
    }
    public static StringBuffer deleteCharAt(StringBuffer sb, int i) {
        return new StringBuffer(deleteCharAt(sb.toString(),i));
    }
    public static void main(String argv[]) {
        String str = argv[0];
        int n = Integer.parseInt(argv[1]);
        str = FixIt1.deleteCharAt(str,n);
        System.out.println(str);
    }
}
```

The class defines a basic static method deleteCharAt() that removes a character designated by the int argument and returns the shortened string. It uses the substring() methods of the String class to do this. The substring() methods can take one or two int arguments. With one argument, it returns the substring from the index point to the end of the string. With two arguments, it returns the substring from the first index to just before the second index.

There is a second method that has exactly the same name, but takes a StringBuffer argument instead. This method simply converts to and from Strings and then calls the first method. Use of the exact same method name like this is called **overloading**. The JVM calls the appropriate method once it has identified the argument type.

Finally, there is a main method, so the program can be run in a standalone fashion as well.

7.3.2 Vector

One of the most useful classes of the java.util package is Vector. The Vector class is very similar to an array, except that its size does not have to be specified in advance. This makes it ideal for storing the contents of a text file for later processing.

As a tradeoff, vectors are a little tricky to work with. Adding or recalling items to or from a vector requires a little more than performing the same actions on an array. The following program shows how the two differ. What it does is read in the same exp.txt file we used to store the materials for the Exp program of chapter 6. It then stores the contents of that file in an array a and a vector v.

The first part of the program does the imports for IO and for the Vector class. Everything takes place in the main method. First, various variables are declared and instantiated:

```
import java.io.*;
import java.util.*;

public class ArrVec {
    public static void main(String argv[]) {
    Vector v = new Vector();
    String a[] = new String[0];
    String line;
    int count = 0;
    . . .
```

The next part of the main method is a try/catch structure. This reads in the contents of the exp.txt file into a string variable line which, in turn, is used to put the contents into the array and vector. Notice that the array must be declared to be of sufficient size. Thus, the first line of the exp.txt file was an explicit count of the number of remaining lines in the file. That number is *not* needed by the Vector class. Notice too that the syntax for adding elements to the two data structures is different. The array uses a simple assignment operator =, while the vector uses the command addElement():

```
    . . .
    try {
        FileReader fr = new FileReader("exp.txt");
        BufferedReader br = new BufferedReader(fr);
        int max = Integer.parseInt(br.readLine());
```

```
    a = new String[max];
    while ((line = br.readLine()) != null) {
        a[count++] = line;
        v.addElement(line);
    }
    br.close();
} catch (Exception e) {
    e.printStackTrace();
}
...
```

The last part of the main method prints out the contents of the array and vector. In the case of the array, this is straightforward. The count variable is reinitialized to zero, and a for structure counts through the members of the array, printing each one.

In the case of the vector, something else must be done. First, we must read the elements of the vector into an instance of Enumeration. The Enumeration is then spooled through using a while structure:

```
System.out.println("array contents");
for (count = 0; count < a.length; count++) {
    System.out.println(a[count]);
}
System.out.println("vector contents");
Enumeration e = v.elements();
while (e.hasMoreElements()) {
        System.out.println((String) e.nextElement());
    }
}
}
```

Notice two things about recalling elements from a vector. First, the syntax is rather similar to, but *not* identical to, that used for StringTokenizer. Second, note that the call to nextElement() must be preceded by (String). This is because the vector is not declared specific to strings, and could, in principle, contain any sort of object. Thus when returning the elements of a vector, you must specify precisely what object it is. This is called **casting**.

As a final point about Vector, the elements it stores must be real objects, and not simple data types. Thus, you *cannot* use a Vector to store simple ints, longs, or chars.[8]

All is not lost, however. Java technology provides **wrapper** classes for all its primitive data types for just this eventuality. So, while you can't put an int directly into a Vector, you can convert an int into its wrapper class Integer. The following sample code shows how to do this. The class begins by declaring and instantiating a vector and then declaring and assigning three ints:

```
import java.util.*;

public class IntVec {
    public static void main(String argv[]) {
        Vector v = new Vector();
        int i = 5;
        int j = 3;
        int k = 17;
        . . .
```

Next the program creates three new Integer objects using the int variables already created, and adds them to the vector:

```
        . . .
        Integer ci = new Integer(i);
        Integer cj = new Integer(j);
        Integer ck = new Integer(k);
        v.addElement(ci);
        v.addElement(cj);
        v.addElement(ck);
        . . .
```

Last, the program uses an Enumeration to retrieve the vector elements. Since they are Integer objects, the result of the nextElement() method must explicitly be cast as an Integer. The Integer then returns an int value with the Integer method intValue():

```
        . . .
        Enumeration e = v.elements();
        while (e.hasMoreElements()) {
            Integer temp = (Integer) e.nextElement();
            int t = temp.intValue();
            System.out.println(t);
        }
    }
}
```

As we've seen, vectors are very useful for file IO. Lines can be read into a vector until the end of the file without having to know in advance how many lines the file will have. I now give a utility program that takes a file as an argument and can be used to return a vector containing the contents of the file. The program is written with a main method so that if run on its own, it will print out the contents of the file. It can also be used as a utility class by other programs, as we'll see later.

The program includes import statements for java.util and java.io. It also declares class-level variables for the vector and for the name of the file to be read:

```
import java.util.*;
import java.io.*;

public class VReader {
    private Vector lines;
    private String filename;
    . . .
```

The constructor for the class takes a string argument and assigns it to the filename variable. It then initializes the vector and calls a method putLines():

```
    . . .
    public VReader(String f) {
        filename = f;
        lines = new Vector();
        putLines();
    }
    . . .
```

The main method calls the constructor with a command-line argument. It creates a vector and assigns it with a call to another method getLines(). It then prints out the contents of the vector:

```
    . . .
    public static void main(String argv[]) {
        VReader vr = new VReader(argv[0]);
        Vector temp = vr.getLines();
        Enumeration e = temp.elements();
        while (e.hasMoreElements()) {
            System.out.println((String) e.nextElement());
        }
    }
    . . .
```

The putLines() method is the substantive one. It does the file IO and reads each line into the vector:

```
    . . .
    private void putLines() {
        String line;
```

```
        try {
            FileReader fr = new FileReader(filename);
            BufferedReader br = new BufferedReader(fr);
            while ((line = br.readLine()) != null) {
                lines.addElement(line);
            }
            br.close();
        } catch (Exception e) {
            e.printStackTrace();
        }
    }
    . . .
```

Finally, the getLines() method provides an accessor for the vector of lines:

```
    . . .
    public Vector getLines() {
        return lines;
    }
    . . .
```

7.3.3   Hashtable

Another extremely useful data structure is Hashtable, which is also part of the java.util package. A **hash** is a data structure rather similar to a vector, except that the individual variables are associated with *objects* – typically strings – rather than indices. Each object – or **key** – of the array can store another object – or **value**. These key–value pairs can be added and removed or iterated through. Here is a simple program that shows how this works.

The program is called HashTest1. There is an import statement, so that Hashtable is available, and then the hash is initialized:

```
import java.util.*;

public class HashTest1 {
    public static void main(String argv[]) {
        Hashtable h = new Hashtable();
        . . .
```

Next, the program initializes three string variables and three Integer objects. Recall that strings are objects too, even though they are not initialized in the same way.[9] Hashes can only operate on objects and that is why the integers are set up as Integer, rather than as int:

```
. . .
String x = "hat";
String y = "zebra";
String z = "orange";
Integer a = new Integer(35);
Integer b = new Integer(10);
Integer c = new Integer(3);
. . .
```

The key–value pairs are then added to the hash with the put() command:

```
. . .
h.put(x,a);
h.put(y,b);
h.put(z,c);
. . .
```

They keys can be invoked directly or retrieved with an Enumeration. We use a while structure to step through the keys of the Enumeration. For each key, we use get() to get the value. Like Vector, the values – and the keys – can be any objects, so they must be explicitly cast as their true object types for the assignments to temp1 and tempInteg to work. Finally, we use a new command toString() to return the string representation of the Integer, so that it can be printed:

```
. . .
Enumeration e = h.keys();
while (e.hasMoreElements()) {
    String temp1 = (String) e.nextElement();
    Integer tempInteg = (Integer) h.get(temp1);
    String temp2 = tempInteg.toString();
    System.out.println(temp1 + ": " + temp2);
  }
 }
}
```

Hashes are extremely useful for text manipulation. They allow us to pair bits of text with any sort of information. We now write a simple concordance program using Hashtable, StringTokenizer, and the VReader program developed in the previous section. A concordance is a list of all the words that occur in some text. Our program also keeps track of the number of occurrences of each word. The basic logic of the program is as follows. First, the contents of a text file are read into a vector by VReader. They are then tokenized by StringTokenizer and each word is made into a new key of a hash with the value 1. As duplicates are found, the value is incremented.

We'll go through the code method by method as usual. First, there are several class-level variables. The hash h will hold the concordance. The vector lines will hold the lines returned by VReader. The constructor itself initializes the hash, calls VReader on its string argument, uses the VReader method getLines() to retrieve the vector of lines, and calls a method makeConc():

```java
import java.util.*;

public class Concord {
    private Hashtable h;
    private Vector lines;
    public Concord(String f) {
        h = new Hashtable();
        VReader vr = new VReader(f);
        lines = vr.getLines();
        makeConc();
    }
    . . .
```

The class can be called via its main method or as a utility class for some other program. If it is called from its main method, then it instantiates the Concord class, and uses a public method getConc() to print out the contents of the hash. As above, this is done by getting an Enumeration of the keys of the hash, and then using a while structure to loop through all the keys. Here we print out the contents of the key (temp1) and the contents of the value (temp2):

```java
    . . .
    public static void main(String argv[]) {
        Concord c = new Concord(argv[0]);
        Hashtable theHash = c.getConc();
        Enumeration e = theHash.keys();
        String temp1, temp2;
        Integer i;
        while (e.hasMoreElements()) {
            temp1 = (String) e.nextElement();
            i = (Integer) theHash.get(temp1);
            temp2 = i.toString();
            System.out.println(temp1 + ":\t" + temp2);
        }
    }
    . . .
```

The heart of the Concord program is the makeConc() method. This method goes through the vector of lines returned from VReader line by line, using a StringTokenizer to break it up into words. In this case, the tokens are defined as anything separated by space, tab, new line, or period (full stop). Each word token is then passed to a new method doConc():

```
. . .
private void makeConc() {
   Enumeration e1 = lines.elements();
   StringTokenizer st;
   String line, word;
   while (e1.hasMoreElements()) {
      line = (String) e1.nextElement();
      st = new StringTokenizer(line," \t\n.");
      while (st.hasMoreTokens()) {
         word = st.nextToken();
         doConc(word);
      }
   }
}
. . .
```

The doConc() method adds elements to the hash with the value 1, or increments the value as appropriate. There is an if structure to test whether the word token is already in the hash as a key. If it is, it is incremented; if not, it is added to the hash with the value 1.[10] The method makes use of the new command containsKey(), which checks if its argument is already a key in the relevant hash:

```
. . .
private void doConc(String w) {
   Integer i;
   if (h.containsKey(w)) {
      i = (Integer) h.get(w);
      int myInt = i.intValue();
      myInt++;
      i = new Integer(myInt);
   } else {
      i = new Integer(1);
   }
   h.put(w,i);
}
. . .
```

Finally, there is a public accessor method for the hash containing the concordance:

```
  . . .
    public Hashtable getConc() {
        return h;
    }
}
```

Running Concord on a text file produces a list of all the words in that file along with the number of times each occurs. Notice that the words are not printed in any particular order. That is, the keys iterated through by Enumeration are not sorted.

If we want the items to be sorted, there are two options here. One possibility would be to write a program to sort the words. It's not hard to do this, although it does take a fair amount of programming sophistication to do it efficiently.

Here's a relatively simple solution, making use of a straightforward (but inefficient) sorting algorithm. The basic idea is to sidestep the main method in the Concord class, using the new main of ConcordCaller instead. Concord is invoked as before, but instead of looping through the randomly ordered keys provided by Enumeration, we make use of a new class FixIt2, which sorts those keys into an array of strings. We step through that array in ConcordCaller. Here is the code for ConcordCaller:

```
import java.util.*;

public class ConcordCaller {
    public static void main(String argv[]) {
        Concord conc = new Concord(argv[0]);
        Hashtable results = conc.getConc();
        String[] myKeys = FixIt2.sortKeys(results);
        for (int i = 0; i < myKeys.length; i++) {
            String theKey = myKeys[i];
            String theValue = ((Integer) results.get(theKey)).toString();
            System.out.println(theKey + ": " + theValue);
        }
    }
}
```

Just for fun, note how we've assigned the value of theValue. In a single statement, we use theKey to retrieve the number of occurrences from results and then – since that number is stored as an Integer – we convert it to a string. In general, you should avoid putting this much in a single command.

This calls a static method sortKeys() in the FixIt2 class. That method first creates an Enumeration of keys to the hash that contains the concordance. Then the keys are transferred to an array. Finally, the nested for loops implement an **insertion sort**. This involves going through the whole array once for each successive string in the array, slowly sorting top down one by one. This is done by adding the built-in String.compareTo() method to the for test-clause. This returns -1 if the string precedes its argument alphabetically. Finally, sortKeys() returns the sorted array:

```java
import java.util.*;

public class FixIt2 {
    public static String[] sortKeys (Hashtable h) {
        int size = h.size();
        Enumeration e = h.keys();
        String[] theKeys = new String[size];
        int j = 0;
        while (e.hasMoreElements()) {
            theKeys[j] = (String) e.nextElement();
            j++;
        }
        j = 0;
        String temp;
        for (int i = 1; i < theKeys.length; i++) {
            temp = theKeys[i];
            for (j = i; j > 0 && temp.compareTo(theKeys[j-1]) < 0; j--) {
                theKeys[j] = theKeys[j-1];
            }
            theKeys[j] = temp;
        }
        return theKeys;
    }
}
```

Another option is to make use of another class from the java.util package: TreeMap. Elements are added to this object exactly like a hash, but when the elements are retrieved, they can be iterated through in alphabetical (or numerical) order. There are two caveats about TreeMap, however. The first is that TreeMap is part of the **collections** system that was only introduced as of Java 1.2. Hence it is not available in earlier versions of Java.[11] The second caveat is that iterating through a TreeMap is a little different from iterating through a Hashtable. The following simple program shows how TreeMap works.

The program first declares and instantiates a TreeMap. It then puts three key–value pairs in it. Just for fun, we've compressed the creation of string and Integer objects here. Since they are not reused, we've simply instantiated them *anonymously* in place, with the new keyword. To step through the keys, we use an Iterator, which is the collections framework equivalent of an Enumeration. The command keySet() returns an ordered set of keys. This set is immediately used to return an Iterator with the command iterator(). We use a while structure to step through the keys in the Iterator:

```java
import java.util.*;

public class TMTest {
    public static void main(String argv[]) {
        TreeMap t = new TreeMap();
        t.put(new String("hat"),new Integer(5));
        t.put(new String("chair"),new Integer(1));
        t.put(new String("people"),new Integer(35));
        Iterator i = t.keySet().iterator();
        while (i.hasNext()) {
            String s = (String) i.next();
            Integer myInt = (Integer) t.get(s);
            System.out.println(s + ":\t" + myInt.toString());
        }
    }
}
```

The commands here are similar, but different from the others we have used in while structures. Let's summarize these different counters and their different behaviors before going on. Vectors and hashes can use an Enumeration object to iterate through their contents. The Enumeration is created with the command elements() or keys(). The StringTokenizer class needs no separate class to iterate. The TreeMap class uses an Iterator object to go through its keys. The Iterator is created with keySet().iterator().

Let's look at the looping for each:

Type	StringTokenizer	Iterator	Enumeration
while-test	hasMoreTokens()	hasNext()	hasMoreElements()
Assignment	nextToken()	next()	nextElement()
Explicit cast	No	Yes	Yes

The table gives each of the three iteration types that we've treated. For each type, the table shows the name of the iteration type, what goes in the while-test, how assignment occurs, and whether an explicit cast is needed.

7.4 Random

The last class I'll treat in this chapter is Random, also from the java.util package. The Random class allows us to generate random numbers. There are a variety of methods available to do this. The following program exemplifies one of the most useful.

The Ran1 program first creates an instance of Random. It then invokes the nextInt() command using the two command-line arguments.[12] The first argument tells Ran1 how many random integers to produce. The second tells it what the range of integers is. The command r.nextInt(limit) returns a random integer between 0 (inclusive) and limit (exclusive):

```java
import java.util.*;

public class Ran1 {
    public static void main(String argv[]) {
        Random r = new Random();
        int max = Integer.parseInt(argv[0]);
        int limit = Integer.parseInt(argv[1]);
        for (int i = 0; i < max; i++) {
            System.out.println(i + ": " + r.nextInt(limit));
        }
    }
}
```

Since Java 1.2, there have been two nextInt() commands. One takes an int argument and is exemplified above. The other takes no argument and returns a random int between −32,768 and 32,767 (the maximum range of an int). To achieve the same functionality in Java 1.1, we can make use of the modulus operator %. Recall that m % n returns the remainder of dividing m by n. Thus, to get a random number between 0 and n, we calculate a random number using the no-argument version of nextInt(). We take the absolute value of that, and then get the remainder of dividing by n.[13] A revision of Ran1 that works like this is given below:

```java
import java.util.*;

public class FixItRan {
    public static void main(String argv[]) {
        Random r = new Random();
        int max = Integer.parseInt(argv[0]);
        int limit = Integer.parseInt(argv[1]);
        int num;
        for (int i = 0; i < max; i++) {
            num = Math.abs(r.nextInt()) % limit;
            System.out.println(i + ": " + num);
        }
    }
}
```

Note that this makes use of the Math.abs() function to return the absolute value of a number.

We can use the Ran1 or FixItRan command to randomize a list of items. I demonstrate this with a program Randomizer, which takes a vector as an argument and returns a scrambled vector. There are two class-level variables for holding the input and output vectors. The constructor assigns its argument to the input vector and initializes the output vector. It then calls the main method of the class: – randomize():

```
import java.util.*;

public class Randomizer {
    Vector input, output;
    public Randomizer(Vector v) {
        input = v;
        output = new Vector();
        randomize();
    }
    . . .
```

The main method allows for Randomizer to be run in a "test" mode with the input vector constructed from command-line arguments. First, the arguments are read into a vector testVec. The Randomizer class is initialized with testVec. The scrambled vector is retrieved with an accessor method getVec(), and the contents of the output vector are printed line by line:

```
    . . .
    public static void main(String argv[]) {
        Vector testVec = new Vector();
        for (int i = 0; i < argv.length; i++) {
            testVec.addElement(argv[i]);
        }
        Randomizer ran = new Randomizer(testVec);
        Vector resVec = ran.getVec();
        Enumeration e = resVec.elements();
        String letter;
        while (e.hasMoreElements()) {
            letter = (String) e.nextElement();
            System.out.println(letter);
        }
    }
    . . .
```

The principal method of Randomizer is randomize(). What it does is step through the input vector with an Enumeration and then add elements from the input vector to the output vector at random points. It does this by means of three critical lines of code within the while structure. The first gets the current size of the output vector. The second generates a random integer between zero and the current size of the output vector, and assigns that value to current. The third inserts the next element from the Enumeration at the point given by current:

```
. . .
private void randomize() {
    Random r = new Random();
    Enumeration e = input.elements();
    String let;
    int max,current;
    while (e.hasMoreElements()) {
        let = (String) e.nextElement();
        max = output.size();
        current = r.nextInt(max + 1);
        output.insertElementAt(let,current);
    }
}
. . .
```

Finally, there is a public accessor method for the output vector:

```
. . .
public Vector getVec() {
    return output;
}
. . .
```

7.5 *Summary*

In this chapter, we covered some of the more useful classes and methods for manipulating text. These provide powerful tools to examine and manipulate textual data. These include the StringBuffer class, which includes a number of methods for altering strings. We also introduced the StringTokenizer class for parsing a string into words.

We introduced the Hashtable class, which we made special use of in our concordance program. Finally, we went over the Random class, which provides for random numbers.

7.6 *Exercises*

1. Amplify the PigLatin program so that it operates on files.
2. Rewrite the PigLatin program above so that it does *not* make use of the StringBuffer class.
3. The letter y is occasionally treated as a vowel in English spelling; for example, in words like "myth" or "my". Revise the PigLatin program so that it deals with y appropriately.
4. The command parseInt() is invoked with the prefix Integer, but the intValue() command is invoked with a specific Integer variable; for example, temp.intValue() in the IntVec program above. Why?
5. Use the TreeMap class to revise Concord.
6. Revise the Materials class of the Exp program of the previous chapter so that the materials are randomized.

Notes

[1] To find out more, you can peruse or even download the *full* API reference documentation from the Java website (http://www.javasoft.com). Access to the API documentation is essential as you progress. It lists all the classes and methods that Java technology provides.

[2] Since Java 1.2.

[3] Also since Java 1.2. I'll have more to say about Swing in appendix A.

[4] As I discuss in more depth in appendix A, Java has undergone some significant changes since its original introduction. Some of the methods introduced in this section only work as of Java 1.2, and will not work in earlier versions.

[5] As a matter of pedantic interest, notice that consonant() treats the letter y as a consonant. This program would thus produce the wrong results for a word such as "myth". Fixing this is left as an exercise.

[6] Note that deleteCharAt() is only available as of Java 1.2. A workaround for Java 1.1 is provided in the next section.

[7] The latter are introduced in chapter 10.

[8] Recall that even though Strings are declared and instantiated just like ints, they are actually objects, while ints are not.

[9] Actually, as objects, Strings can actually be initialized in usual object fashion – for example, String x = new String("hat"); – which does the same thing as String x = "hat";.

[10] If you attempt to add a new key–value pair to a hash where that key is already present, the original key–value pair is wiped out by the later one.

[11] I discuss the different versions of the Java language in appendix A.

[12] This command is not available in Java 1.1. A workaround is provided below.

[13] This may be more math than you want to know about. If so, take my word that this little procedure works!

Chapter 8

Graphical User Interfaces

Most modern software uses a **graphical user interface** (GUI), allowing the user to click and point, rather than type out commands. In this chapter, I introduce the Java™ machinery to do this, augmenting some of the programs previously introduced with a simple standalone GUI.[1] This is a huge and complex topic, but if you want to write programs that are easy to use, you need to know something about it.

8.1 Components and Events

A graphical user interface – or GUI – is a scheme whereby a user can interact with a program in a graphical fashion. What this usually means is pointing and clicking rather than typing. Up to this point, I have eased our introduction to Java technology by using a very old-fashioned text-based interface. The user can enter information by command-line arguments, by entering text at the prompt, or by file input.

   With a GUI, the user can enter information in other ways. He or she can click buttons of various types, select items from lists, and use the mouse to select or draw. This is a good thing from a number of perspectives. With more ways to input information, the program can be more powerful. Moreover, the interface can be more intuitive and easier for a new user to make sense of. All this power comes with a cost, of course. Developing a GUI requires knowledge of new classes and methods.

   The basic idea behind a Java GUI has three parts: **containers, components**, and **events**. Loosely, containers are graphical objects that can contain things. For example, windows are a common container. Windows can contain menus, buttons, text, and so on. Another container that is quite important for the Java language is the applet. Components are the GUI objects that windows can contain; for example, buttons, checkboxes, menus, text fields of various sorts, and so on. Finally, events are what happens when some sort of activity takes place with respect to some component or container.

Building a GUI involves selecting the appropriate container(s) and components, and determining what actions take place when. This is done by attaching a **listener** to the relevant component. For example, if one wants to write a GUI that involves some sort of input via a button, it would be done as follows. The general container is declared; for example, some sort of window. A button is declared and added to that container. A listener is added to that button, and code is written in the listener for what happens when the button is pressed.

Let's begin with a simple example. Let's construct a little window that closes when the close box (in the upper left or right) is clicked. We need two classes to do this. The first is called CloseFrame and constructs the window itself. First, it uses graphics classes and methods, and must import them from the java.awt package. As is very common for graphics programs, it has to extend (or inherit from) an existing graphics object, in this case, Frame. We will always invoke Frame when we need a basic window. The constructor first constructs the window-closing class Closer. It then applies the command addWindowListener() with the Closer as an argument. This command tells the Java program that Closer will handle events dealing with the window as a whole. Next, the size of the window is set. The arguments to setSize() are in horizontal and vertical pixels. Finally, the command show() forces the window to be visible:

```
import java.awt.*;

public class CloseFrame extends Frame {
    public CloseFrame() {
        Closer c = new Closer();
        addWindowListener(c);
        setSize(300,300);
        show();
    }
    public static void main(String argv[]) {
        CloseFrame cf = new CloseFrame();
    }
}
```

The Closer class extends a class WindowAdapter which allows for a specified set of methods to respond to window-level events. Since events are referred to in the class, it must import from the java.awt.event subpackage. The Closer class defines only one method: windowClosing(). The System.exit(0) command forces the program to terminate when the close-box is clicked:

```
import java.awt.event.*;

public class Closer extends WindowAdapter {
   public void windowClosing(WindowEvent e) {
      System.exit(0);
   }
}
```

There is another method for dealing with component–listener pairings, and this is to make use of **interfaces**. In chapter 6, I introduced objects and inheritance. The keyword extends is used to stipulate that some class inherits the methods and variables of another class. For example, the Closer class above inherits from the WindowAdapter class, and CloseFrame inherits from Frame.

Interfaces are somewhat different. When we specify that some class implements an interface, what we mean is that the former provides definitions for specific methods that the interface class specifies. To implement an interface is to inherit *nothing* in fact.

Events can also be handled with interfaces. For example, the CloseFrame class can be rewritten using a WindowListener interface, rather than a separate WindowAdapter class, as follows. The new program is called CloseFrameInt. It inherits from Frame, but implements the WindowListener interface. Implementing the latter requires that the CloseFrameInt class include the seven methods that WindowListener requires, which stipulate what happens when various window events occur. All of these methods occur in CloseFrameInt, but only windowClosing() is fleshed out. Notice how the addWindowListener() command takes the keyword this, indicating that the Frame is its own WindowListener:

```
import java.awt.*;
import java.awt.event.*;

public class CloseFrameInt extends Frame implements WindowListener {
   public CloseFrameInt() {
      addWindowListener(this);
      setSize(300,300);
      show();
   }
   public void windowClosing(WindowEvent e) {
      System.exit(0);
   }
   public void windowActivated(WindowEvent e) {}
   public void windowClosed(WindowEvent e) {}
```

```
    public void windowDeactivated(WindowEvent e) {}
    public void windowDeiconified(WindowEvent e) {}
    public void windowIconified(WindowEvent e) {}
    public void windowOpened(WindowEvent e) {}
    public static void main(String argv[]) {
        CloseFrame cf = new CloseFrame();
    }
}
```

You might think that since implementing the WindowListener requires all these methods, that it would be simpler to extend WindowAdapter. The problem with that is that, as we already mentioned above, a class can only extend *one* class.[2] Hence, if CloseFrame, or CloseFrameInt, extends Frame, it cannot also extend WindowAdapter.

8.2   *Laying Things Out*

Let's now consider how to add components to a container. The key intermediate device is the Layout. GUI components can be laid out in a variety of ways:

FlowLayout   This is the default layout for Panel. It places things left to right, top to bottom.

BorderLayout   This is the default layout for Frame. It defines four border areas in the container – "North", "South", "East", and "West" – plus "Center".

GridLayout   This layout sets up a specified number of rows and columns and places components in those.

CardLayout   This layout allows you to have different components trade off in the same container space.

GridbagLayout   This layout is a more sophisticated version of the GridLayout above, where the cells defined by the rows and columns need not have the same size.

I will only treat the FlowLayout and BorderLayout classes, as they are the most useful and the easiest to learn. I will exemplify each with various GUI components in the next section.

8.3   *Some Useful Controls*

In this section, I will go through the most useful control components.

8.3.1   Buttons

To see how the layouts affect the placement of a component, let's turn to the most useful component: Button. The sample code below adds a button to the CloseFrameInt program that we have already written above. The code here is exactly the same as for CloseFrameInt, except that a button has been declared and initialized. The argument to the button's constructor determines the message that the button displays. After the button is initialized, it is added. Since the default layout for a Frame is BorderLayout, we can explicitly add the button to one of the five areas defined by BorderLayout. The area is capitalized, surrounded by quotes, and comes first before the component being added:

```
import java.awt.*;
import java.awt.event.*;

public class ButtonEx1 extends Frame implements WindowListener {
   Button b;
   public ButtonEx1() {
      addWindowListener(this);
      setSize(300,300);
      b = new Button("Do nothing");
      add("East",b);
      show();
   }
   public void windowClosing(WindowEvent e) {
      System.exit(0);
   }
   public void windowActivated(WindowEvent e) {}
   public void windowClosed(WindowEvent e) {}
   public void windowDeactivated(WindowEvent e) {}
   public void windowDeiconified(WindowEvent e) {}
   public void windowIconified(WindowEvent e) {}
   public void windowOpened(WindowEvent e) {}
   public static void main(String argv[]) {
      ButtonEx1 be = new ButtonEx1();
   }
}
```

This program displays the following window and button:

Here, the button fills the entire "East" sector of the Frame.

If we wanted to display the button using a different layout, there are two choices. One possibility is to set a new layout for the Frame. This is what we do in ButtonEx2. The command to change the layout is setLayout() and it takes a layout object as an argument. Here the FlowLayout is declared anonymously:

```java
import java.awt.*;
import java.awt.event.*;

public class ButtonEx2 extends Frame implements WindowListener {
    Button b;
    public ButtonEx2() {
        addWindowListener(this);
        setSize(300,300);
        setLayout(new FlowLayout());
        b = new Button("Do nothing");
        add(b);
        show();
    }
    public void windowClosing(WindowEvent e) {
        System.exit(0);
    }
    public void windowActivated(WindowEvent e) {}
    public void windowClosed(WindowEvent e) {}
    public void windowDeactivated(WindowEvent e) {}
    public void windowDeiconified(WindowEvent e) {}
    public void windowIconified(WindowEvent e) {}
    public void windowOpened(WindowEvent e) {}
    public static void main(String argv[]) {
        ButtonEx2 be = new ButtonEx2();
    }
}
```

This produces the following display:

Another possibility is to add a Panel to the Frame, and then add the button to the Panel. A Panel is simply a named area of a container. It can be used as a convenient **subcontainer**. Since the default layout for a Panel is FlowLayout, this has the same result:

```java
import java.awt.*;
import java.awt.event.*;

public class ButtonEx3 extends Frame implements WindowListener {
    Button b;
    public ButtonEx3() {
        addWindowListener(this);
        setSize(300,300);
        Panel p = new Panel();
        b = new Button("Do nothing");
        p.add(b);
        add(p);
        show();
    }
    public void windowClosing(WindowEvent e) {
        System.exit(0);
    }
    public void windowActivated(WindowEvent e) {}
    public void windowClosed(WindowEvent e) {}
    public void windowDeactivated(WindowEvent e) {}
    public void windowDeiconified(WindowEvent e) {}
    public void windowIconified(WindowEvent e) {}
    public void windowOpened(WindowEvent e) {}
    public static void main(String argv[]) {
        ButtonEx3 be = new ButtonEx3();
    }
}
```

The sole effect of adding the Panel here is to change the layout that the Button is added with. This results in the same display as ButtonEx2 above. More complex effects can be obtained with Panels when we take into consideration that they too can have layouts. Note that adding a component in a BorderLayout without specifying any particular zone defaults to "Center".

Notice the syntax for the add() commands. When specified without a preceding object (and dot), it takes the current object – the Frame here – as what is being added to. Otherwise, if there is a preceding object as in p.add(b) above, it takes that object as the container (the Panel in this case).

Now that we know how to add a Button, let's go on to have our Button do something. A button-pressing event is handled by an ActionListener interface. The ActionListener interface requires only one method actionPerformed(). (Since the interface is so simple, there is no independent "ActionAdapter" class.) The following example shows how it works:

```java
import java.awt.*;
import java.awt.event.*;

public class ButtonEx4 extends Frame implements ActionListener {
    Button b;
    int i;
    public ButtonEx4() {
        i = 1;
        addWindowListener(new Closer());
        setSize(300,300);
        setLayout(new FlowLayout());
        b = new Button("Press me!");
        b.addActionListener(this);
        add(b);
        show();
    }
    public void actionPerformed(ActionEvent e) {
        System.out.println("Button press #" + i++);
    }
    public static void main(String argv[]) {
        ButtonEx4 be = new ButtonEx4();
    }
}
```

This example handles windowClosing() events with the separate Closer class, rather than by implementing the WindowListener interface directly. I do this so that the ActionListener code is as clear as possible. This program defines and instantiates a Button, just as in the previous examples. The class as a whole implements an ActionListener interface, which requires that it include the actionPerformed() method. We must explicitly add the listener to the button with the addActionListener() command, which does so with the this keyword, since the class is its own ActionListener. In this case, pressing the button simply prints a message that indicates how many times the button has been pressed.

Recall that even though a class may only extend or inherit from a single class, it may implement any number of interfaces. The program below behaves exactly like ButtonEx4, except that it implements a WindowListener instead of calling a WindowAdapter. The program differs from the previous one in several ways. First, it explicitly implements *two* interfaces (separated by a comma). It then adds both listeners with the keyword this, since both listeners are part of the same class:

```java
import java.awt.*;
import java.awt.event.*;

public class ButtonEx5 extends Frame
    implements WindowListener, ActionListener {
  Button b;
  int i;
  public ButtonEx5() {
    i = 1;
    addWindowListener(this);
    setLayout(new FlowLayout());
    setSize(300,300);
    b = new Button("Press me!");
    b.addActionListener(this);
    add(b);
    show();
  }
  . . .
```

The remainder of the program includes the required methods from both interfaces and the main method:

```java
  . . .
  public void actionPerformed(ActionEvent e) {
    System.out.println("Button press #" + i++);
  }
  public void windowClosing(WindowEvent e) {
    System.exit(0);
  }
  public void windowActivated(WindowEvent e) {}
  public void windowClosed(WindowEvent e) {}
  public void windowDeactivated(WindowEvent e) {}
```

```
        public void windowDeiconified(WindowEvent e) {}
        public void windowIconified(WindowEvent e) {}
        public void windowOpened(WindowEvent e) {}
        public static void main(String argv[]) {
            ButtonEx5 be = new ButtonEx5();
        }
    }
```

We must also allow for multiple buttons. The way this works is that each button defines an ActionCommand which is available to the actionPerformed() method. By default, the name appearing on the button is the ActionCommand, but any string can be specified as a button's ActionCommand, with the command setActionCommand(). The following program exemplifies this with three buttons.

The constructor for the program instantiates three buttons and adds them to the Frame. The constructor also includes a rather silly setActionCommand() statement for b2. The upshot is that the ActionCommands for the three buttons are 1, hat, and 3 respectively:

```
import java.awt.*;
import java.awt.event.*;

public class ButtonEx6 extends Frame implements ActionListener {
    Button b1,b2,b3;
    public ButtonEx6() {
        addWindowListener(new Closer());
        setSize(300,300);
        setLayout(new FlowLayout());
        b1 = new Button("1");
        b2 = new Button("2");
        b3 = new Button("3");
        b1.addActionListener(this);
        b2.addActionListener(this);
        b3.addActionListener(this);
        b2.setActionCommand("hat");
        add(b1);
        add(b2);
        add(b3);
        show();
    }
    . . .
```

The actionPerformed() method shows how the different buttons are responded to. First we use the getActionCommand(), applied to the ActionEvent argument, to retrieve the ActionCommand associated with the event. We then use an if structure to selectively respond to each different button press. In this case, an appropriate message is printed:

```
    . . .
    public void actionPerformed(ActionEvent e) {
        String temp = e.getActionCommand();
        if (temp.equals("1")) {
            System.out.println("Button 1 pressed.");
        } else if (temp.equals("hat")) {
            System.out.println("Button 2 pressed.");
        } else {
            System.out.println("Button 3 pressed.");
        }
    }
    public static void main(String argv[]) {
        ButtonEx6 be = new ButtonEx6();
    }
}
```

8.3.2   Menus

One extremely useful control is a Menu. The important thing to remember about Menus in Java is that they have a number of parts, all of which must be present for the Menu to operate properly. First, there must be a MenuBar to place the Menus on. Next, there must be individual Menus, with individual MenuItems. Lastly, an ActionListener must be added to each Menu, which responds to ActionCommands defined by each MenuItem. The following program provides a simple example.

The program first declares a MenuBar, Menu, and two MenuItems. The constructor initializes all of these and assigns ActionCommands to the MenuItems. It sets up the MenuBar with the setMenuBar() command and then adds everything together. Finally, it adds the ActionListener to the Menu, not the individual MenuItems:

```
import java.awt.*;
import java.awt.event.*;

public class MenuEx1 extends Frame implements ActionListener {
    MenuBar mb;
    Menu m1;
    MenuItem mi1, mi2;
    public MenuEx1() {
        setSize(300,200);
        addWindowListener(new Closer());
        mb = new MenuBar();
```

```
        m1 = new Menu("Test Menu");
        mi1 = new MenuItem("Item #1");
        mi2 = new MenuItem("Item #2");
        mi1.setActionCommand("1");
        mi2.setActionCommand("2");
        m1.add(mi1);
        m1.add(mi2);
        m1.addActionListener(this);
        mb.add(m1);
        setMenuBar(mb);
        show();
    }
    . . .
```

The actionPerformed() method simply prints out the ActionCommand:

```
    . . .
    public void actionPerformed(ActionEvent e) {
        System.out.println(e.getActionCommand());
    }
    public static void main(String argv[]) {
        new MenuEx1();
    }
  }
```

Setting up the actionPerformed() method so that it responds to individual MenuItems is analogous to responding to individual buttons.

8.3.3   Choices

Another extremely useful control is Choice, which presents a list of items to choose from. Unlike the two previous controls, however, its events are treated with an ItemListener, rather than an ActionListener. The ItemListener interface requires only one method itemStateChanged(), and there is therefore no analogous "ItemAdapter" class. The Choice control is made up of a set of items, one of which can be selected. When an ItemEvent is generated, it can be queried for what item of the Choice is selected, and an appropriate action can be taken. The following program exemplifies this.

The class inherits from Frame as usual, but implements the ItemListener interface. A Choice is declared as a class-level variable. The constructor does the usual things for the Frame, and then initializes the Choice object. It then adds three items that can be selected. Note that the proper command here is addItem(), not simply add(). The ItemListener is added to the Choice with the expected addItemListener():

```
import java.awt.*;
import java.awt.event.*;

public class ChoiceEx1 extends Frame implements ItemListener {
    Choice c;
    public ChoiceEx1() {
        setSize(300,200);
        setLayout(new FlowLayout());
        addWindowListener(new Closer());
        c = new Choice();
        c.addItem("hat");
        c.addItem("chair");
        c.addItem("purple");
        c.addItemListener(this);
        add(c);
        show();
    }
    . . .
```

The interface requires the single method itemStateChanged(). I've made the example a little redundant here to demonstrate the two methods for recovering which item from the Choice is selected. One possibility is to retrieve the choice by its index (the set of which are numbered from zero) with the command getSelectedIndex(). The other possibility is to obtain the name of the item selected with getSelectedItem(). Here, we do both:

```
    . . .
    public void itemStateChanged(ItemEvent e) {
        int item = c.getSelectedIndex();
        switch (item) {
            case 0:
                System.out.println("clothing: " + c.getSelectedItem());
                break;
            case 1:
                System.out.println("furniture: " + c.getSelectedItem());
                break;
            default:
                System.out.println("color: " + c.getSelectedItem());
        }
    }
    public static void main(String argv[]) {
        new ChoiceEx1();
    }
}
```

Here is a picture of the Choice control that this produces:

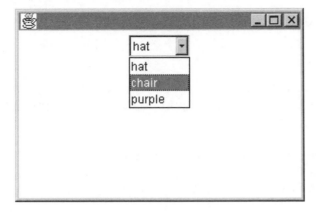

8.3.4   Checkboxes

As a final example of a useful control component, there is the Checkbox. This control places a set of labeled checkboxes on the screen. Like the Choice control, Checkbox uses the ItemListener interface to handle its events. Here is an example. Here three Checkboxes are declared and initialized. The first two are initialized in a CheckboxGroup. This grouping allows the boxes to be mutually exclusive. The third box is outside the group which means that whether it is selected has no effect on the other two boxes. The constructor for a Checkbox includes a boolean variable, which specifies whether the box first appears selected (true) or unselected (false):

```java
import java.awt.*;
import java.awt.event.*;

public class ChboxEx1 extends Frame implements ItemListener {
    Checkbox a,b,c;
    CheckboxGroup cbg;
    public ChboxEx1() {
        setSize(300,200);
        setLayout(new FlowLayout());
        addWindowListener(new Closer());
        cbg = new CheckboxGroup();
        a = new Checkbox("a",cbg,false);
        b = new Checkbox("b",cbg,false);
        c = new Checkbox("c",false);
        a.addItemListener(this);
        b.addItemListener(this);
        c.addItemListener(this);
        add(a);
        add(b);
```

```
      add(c);
      show();
   }
   . . .
```

Here, we respond to a change of state by directly querying the Checkboxes to see if they are selected. If so, an appropriate message is printed:

```
   . . .
   public void itemStateChanged(ItemEvent e) {
      if (a.getState()) {
         System.out.println("a is selected.");
      }
      if (b.getState()) {
         System.out.println("b is selected.");
      }
      if (c.getState()) {
         System.out.println("c is selected.");
      }
   }
   public static void main(String argv[]) {
      new ChboxEx1();
   }
}
```

This is what the program looks like:

8.4   Some Useful Displays

In this section, I go over the various components for displaying text. The three most useful ones are Label, TextField, and TextArea. Here is a picture of all three:

A Label provides for a single line of uneditable text. A TextField or TextArea provide for editable text, either a single line or multiple lines respectively. Here's the program that generated these objects. A Label is instantiated with a string argument. A TextField takes a string argument and an optional int argument specifying the number of columns:

```java
import java.awt.*;

public class Displays extends Frame {
    public Displays() {
        setLayout(new FlowLayout());
        addWindowListener(new Closer());
        Label l = new Label("I'm a label.");
        add(l);
        TextField tf = new TextField("I'm a textfield.");
        add(tf);
        TextArea ta = new TextArea("I'm a textarea.",3,20,
            TextArea.SCROLLBARS_BOTH);
        add(ta);
        pack();
        show();
    }
    public static void main(String argv[]) {
        new Displays();
    }
}
```

A TextArea can be instantiated in several ways: (i) with no arguments; (ii) with a string argument; (iii) with two int arguments, that designate the number of rows and columns respectively; (iv) with a string and two int arguments; and (v) with a string, two ints, and a special constant argument that specifies whether there are scrollbars. For the latter, there are four choices:

- TextArea.SCROLLBARS_BOTH
- TextArea.SCROLLBARS_HORIZONTAL_ONLY
- TextArea.SCROLLBARS_NONE
- TextArea.SCROLLBARS_VERTICAL_ONLY

The only other novel bit of code above is the pack() statement instead of an explicit setSize() statement. Since the sizes of the text components in the example above are all fixed, we can let the window take its natural size; that is, just big enough to display its components comfortably. The pack() statement does this.

All three of the text components here can use the setText() and getText() methods. In addition, TextArea and TextField are both optionally editable; this can be set with the command setEditable(), which takes a boolean argument. The following example shows how these work. This program has a TextField, a Label, and a Button. The TextField is editable (by default) and when the button is pressed, the contents of the TextField are assigned to the Label. Since this can result in the Label changing its size, we use the validate() command, which causes the program to lay out the components again (using the specified layout).

As usual, the program must implement an ActionListener interface to handle the button events:

```
import java.awt.*;
import java.awt.event.*;

public class TextEx1 extends Frame implements ActionListener {
    Label l;
    TextField tf;
    Button b;
    public TextEx1() {
        setSize(300,200);
        setLayout(new FlowLayout());
        addWindowListener(new Closer());
        tf = new TextField("Edit this field.");
        add(tf);
        l = new Label("I'm a label.");
        add(l);
        b = new Button("Copy");
        b.addActionListener(this);
        add(b);
        show();
    }
    . . .
```

The actionPerformed() method is straightforward. First, the contents of the TextField are obtained. Next, they are assigned to the Label. Finally, the components are laid out anew:

```
    . . .
    public void actionPerformed(ActionEvent e) {
        String temp = tf.getText();
```

```
        l.setText(temp);
        validate();
    }
    public static void main(String argv[]) {
        new TextEx1();
    }
}
```

These components can also display different fonts and styles. I treat fonts in section 9.2, below after treating graphics more generally.

8.5   *Some Useful Windows*

There are four window-type environments. I treat Applet in chapter 10, and I have treated Frame above. The other two are Dialog and FileDialog. Both of them are useful for displaying or collecting some tidbit of information in a smaller floating window.

8.5.1   Dialogs

Here's an example of a simple Dialog. First, there is Frame that presents two buttons and a Label:

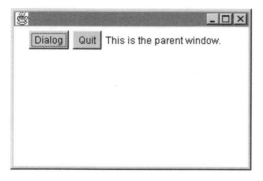

The second button quits the program; the first button brings up the following simple Dialog window:

Clicking on either button dismisses the Dialog, and assigns an appropriate message to the Label in the first window.

Let's now go through the code that produced this. There are two classes, one for the main window DialogFrame and one for the dialog window MyDialog. Let's go through the main window code first. The program declares and instantiates two buttons and a label. It implements an ActionListener for the buttons (note that, for no essential reason, it does not call the Closer class or implement a WindowListener interface – closing of the window and program is handled by the second button):

```
import java.awt.*;
import java.awt.event.*;

public class DialogFrame extends Frame implements ActionListener {
    Button b1,b2;
    Label l;
    public DialogFrame() {
        setSize(300,200);
        setLayout(new FlowLayout());
        b1 = new Button("Dialog");
        b2 = new Button("Quit");
        l = new Label("This is the parent window.");
        b1.addActionListener(this);
        b2.addActionListener(this);
        add(b1);
        add(b2);
        add(l);
        show();
    }
    . . .
```

The first button creates the dialog window. Note that dialogs *must* be called with a Frame argument.[3]

```
    . . .
    public void actionPerformed(ActionEvent e) {
        String temp = e.getActionCommand();
        if (temp.equals("Dialog")) {
            new MyDialog(this);
        } else {
            System.exit(0);
        }
    }
    public static void main(String argv[]) {
```

```
      new DialogFrame();
    }
  }
```

The code for MyDialog is fairly straightforward as well. Much of the code that determines the properties of a Frame also applies to a Dialog. The MyDialog class inherits from Dialog and implements an ActionListener interface to handle button events. It defines two buttons and a variable for its parent Frame. Note that it must call its superclass's constructor as the first command of its own constructor with super(f,true). The second argument here makes it so that the dialog window has control. Nothing can be input into other windows while the dialog window is present:

```
import java.awt.*;
import java.awt.event.*;

public class MyDialog extends Dialog implements ActionListener {
    Button a,b;
    DialogFrame parent;
    public MyDialog(DialogFrame f) {
        super(f,true);
        parent = f;
        setSize(100,100);
        setLayout(new FlowLayout());
        a = new Button("A");
        b = new Button("B");
        a.addActionListener(this);
        b.addActionListener(this);
        add(a);
        add(b);
        show();
    }
    . . .
```

The name of the button is then passed to the Label in the parent class; that is, the Frame that was passed as an argument to the constructor. To close the dialog window without exiting the program, we use dispose():

```
    . . .
    public void actionPerformed(ActionEvent e) {
        parent.l.setText("You pressed button: " + e.getActionCommand());
        dispose();
    }
}
```

8.5.2   FileDialogs

The FileDialog class is an extremely useful one. Unlike the Dialog class it is easily usable directly, without subclassing. Here is an example that uses it to read the contents of a text file into a TextArea. The program has three buttons and a TextArea. The first button creates a FileDialog, which is used to find a text file. That file is then read into the TextArea. The second button clears the TextArea, and the third button quits the program. Here is a screen shot of the program displaying its own code in the TextArea:

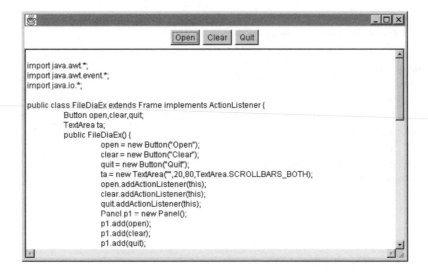

The program is actually relatively straightforward. It imports from the usual packages plus java.io to handle reading from the file. At the class level, there are three buttons and the TextArea. The constructor initializes the components and also adds a Panel. This is so that the components are placed properly. The three buttons are added to the Panel, which has a default FlowLayout. The Panel and TextArea are then added to the "North" and "Center" of the Frame's BorderLayout. Note that the TextArea is set to be uneditable with the command setEditable(false):

```
import java.awt.*;
import java.awt.event.*;
import java.io.*;

public class FileDiaEx extends Frame implements ActionListener {
    Button open,clear,quit;
    TextArea ta;
    public FileDiaEx() {
        open = new Button("Open");
```

```
        clear = new Button("Clear");
        quit = new Button("Quit");
        ta = new TextArea(" ",20,80,TextArea.SCROLLBARS_BOTH);
        ta.setEditable(false);
        open.addActionListener(this);
        clear.addActionListener(this);
        quit.addActionListener(this);
        Panel p1 = new Panel();
        p1.add(open);
        p1.add(clear);
        p1.add(quit);
        add("North",p1);
        add("Center",ta);
        pack();
        show();
    }
    . . .
```

The button events are handled in the obvious way. The "Quit" button quits the program. The "Clear" button sets the text of the TextArea to null. Finally, the "Open" button is complex enough that we handle that in a separate method readTheFile():

```
    . . .
    public void actionPerformed(ActionEvent e) {
        String temp = e.getActionCommand();
        if (temp.equals("Open")) {
            readTheFile();
        } else if (temp.equals("Clear")) {
            ta.setText("");
        } else {
            System.exit(0);
        }
    }
    . . .
```

The readTheFile() method creates and shows the FileDialog. The file and its directory are returned by the methods getFile() and getDirectory(). We then define string variables to hold the contents of the current line of the file and to augment line by line:

```
    . . .
    private void readTheFile() {
        FileDialog fd = new FileDialog(this);
        fd.show();
```

```
        String filename = fd.getFile();
        String dir = fd.getDirectory();
        String fileContents = "";
        String line = "";
        try {
            FileReader fr = new FileReader(dir + filename);
            BufferedReader br = new BufferedReader(fr);
            while ((line = br.readLine()) != null) {
                fileContents = fileContents + "\n" + line;
            }
            br.close();
        } catch (Exception e) {
            fileContents = "File not readable!";
        }
        ta.setText(fileContents);
    }
    . . .
```

Notice how the catch-clause is handled. Instead of printing the error message on the screen, the error is displayed in the TextArea as well. This program is thus completely graphical. After calling the program, nothing is entered or displayed on the command line.

The main method is given below, but it is as usual:

```
    . . .
    public static void main(String argv[]) {
        new FileDiaEx();
    }
}
```

8.6   *Summary*

Let's briefly summarize what we've covered in this chapter. The basic machinery behind a GUI includes containers, control and display components, and events.

The containers are windows of various sorts. I've discussed three. First, there are Frames, which are essentially equivalent to a full-scale window. They can generate events of their own, which are handled by a WindowListener interface or a WindowAdapter class. There are also Dialog windows. These can contain any of the usual control or display components and the events generated by those are handled in the usual fashion. Finally, there is the FileDialog, a specialized dialog window for collecting a filename.

I've presented four control components. Buttons and Menus are the most intuitive and their events are handled by an ActionListener. I also showed how to use Choices and Checkboxes, which both generate events that are handled with an ItemListener.

Last, I've discussed three display components. The Label component displays a single line of uneditable text. A TextField allows for a single line of editable text. Last, a TextArea displays multi-line text with or without scrollbars.

8.7 Exercises

1. Just for fun, write a program that uses *all* of the GUI components.
2. Revise the GrepOO program so that it uses a GUI. (*Hint*: you might want to make use of code from the FileDiaEx program.)
3. Rewrite the Concord program so that it uses a GUI.

Notes

[1] There have been a lot of changes in the GUI packages in the different versions of the Java technology. In this chapter – as in the preceding ones – we stick to Java 1.1.

[2] A class can, however, implement any number of interfaces.

[3] This will be an important point when we go through applets in chapter 10.

Chapter 9
Graphics

A picture is worth a thousand words, and occasionally it is necessary to provide a graphical output to some program. In this chapter, I go over some of the graphics classes and methods that Java™ technology provides.

Whenever a container is resized or shown on the screen, Java does two things. One is to position any components in the container. The second is to *repaint* the container. Repainting means redrawing all the graphics that are in the container.

The way this is implemented is that every container automatically has a paint() method, which can be overridden to place graphical objects in the container. Here is the simplest possible example. This example shows how to draw a few graphical objects in a Frame. The program simply overrides the paint() method and adds commands for drawing three objects. Here's the display:

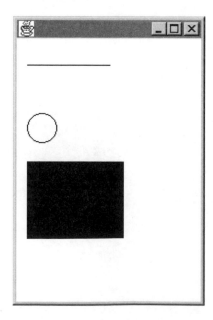

The code is straightforward. A Frame is constructed, which calls Closer to handle window-closing. It overrides the paint() method. That method takes as an argument a Graphics object. That object has a number of methods associated with it for drawing things. This program exemplifies three of them: drawLine(), drawOval(), and fillRect(). All of these methods take pixel locations as arguments. For example, the drawLine() method takes four integer arguments as follows – horizontal location of start point, vertical location of start point, horizontal location of end point, and vertical location of end point:

```java
import java.awt.*;
import java.awt.event.*;

public class GrEx1 extends Frame {
    public GrEx1() {
        setSize(200,300);
        addWindowListener(new Closer());
        show();
    }
    public void paint(Graphics g) {
        g.drawLine(15,50,100,50);
        g.drawOval(15,100,30,30);
        g.fillRect(15,150,100,80);
    }
    public static void main(String argv[]) {
        new GrEx1();
    }
}
```

Here is a list of a few of the more useful Graphics methods. Integer variables x and y always refer to coordinates on a cartesian plane:

```
drawArc(int x, int y, int width, int height,
    int startAngle, int arcAngle)
drawLine(int x1, int y1, int x2, int y2)
drawOval(int x, int y, int width, int height)
drawPolygon(int[] xPoints, int[] yPoints,
    int nPoints)
drawRect(int x, int y, int width, int height)
drawRoundRect(int x, int y, int width, int height,
    int arcWidth, int arcHeight)
drawString(String str, int x, int y)
fillArc(int x, int y, int width, int height,
    int startAngle, int arcAngle)
fillOval(int x, int y, int width, int height)
fillPolygon(int[] xPoints, int[] yPoints,
```

```
    int nPoints)
fillRect(int x, int y, int width, int height)
fillRoundRect(int x, int y, int width, int height,
    int arcWidth, int arcHeight)
```

To get a sense of the coordinate space that you can draw in, the following program uses mouse clicks to draw a point and simultaneously display the coordinates at which the mouse was clicked. This program makes use of a new listener interface, MouseListener, which handles mouse events. The MouseListener interface requires five methods, and there is a corresponding MouseAdapter class that only requires any one of those methods. Here's what the output of the program looks like:

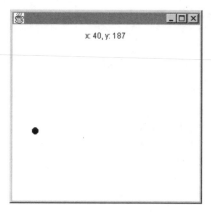

The code is relatively straightforward, but includes some new features. First, the class extends the Frame class, and includes the usual code to size, display, and handle the window-closing event. The program uses a MouseListener interface, and thus includes the five methods that interface requires. At the class level, there are three variables: a Label and two integer variables to hold the coordinate values. In the constructor, the MouseListener is added, and the Label is initialized. There's one additional new command here, setAlignment(), which allows us to set the alignment of text in the Label to LEFT, RIGHT, or CENTER:

```
import java.awt.*;
import java.awt.event.*;

public class MouseGraph extends Frame implements MouseListener {
    Label l;
    int x,y;
    public MouseGraph() {
        setSize(300,300);
```

```
        x = 150;
        y = 150;
        setLayout(new FlowLayout());
        addWindowListener(new Closer());
        addMouseListener(this);
        l = new Label("Click in the window.");
        l.setAlignment(Label.CENTER);
        add(l);
        show();
    }
    . . .
```

Since we are using graphics, we override the paint() method, using the fillOval() command to draw a ball on the screen. Note that fillOval() makes use of the x and y variables defined above to position the oval, and two more int arguments to set its size:

```
    . . .
    public void paint(Graphics g) {
        g.fillOval(x-5,y-5,10,10);
    }
    . . .
```

The mouseClicked() method is where the work gets done. Clicking the mouse anywhere in the Frame, except in the Label, passes a MouseEvent to this method. We can query the event for its coordinates which are assigned to the integer variables we set up. Finally, the method calls the extremely important command repaint(). This causes the current container's paint() method to execute, which it will now do with the *new* coordinate values:

```
    . . .
    public void mouseClicked(MouseEvent e) {
        x = e.getX();
        y = e.getY();
        l.setText("x: " + x + ", y: " + y);
        repaint();
    }
    public void mouseEntered(MouseEvent e) {}
    public void mouseExited(MouseEvent e) {}
    public void mousePressed(MouseEvent e) {}
    public void mouseReleased(MouseEvent e) {}
    public static void main(String argv[]) {
        new MouseGraph();
    }
}
```

9.1   Color

Let's now add color to our programs. All of the components can be specified for colors, as can the background of the various containers. In addition, all of the graphics draw- and fill- commands can be specified for colors. The Java language allows for any color that can be specified in **RGB** (red–green–blue) color space. A number of colors are predefined, however, and for most linguistic purposes, these are more than sufficient. The predefined colors are as follows:

```
Color.black
Color.blue
Color.cyan
Color.darkGray
Color.gray
Color.green
Color.lightGray
Color.magenta
Color.orange
Color.pink
Color.red
Color.white
Color.yellow
```

The following program shows how these can be used to set the background color of a Frame. The program presents a window with a button. Pressing the button toggles through the colors listed. First, the program initializes an array of colors. Notice that an array can be assigned a list of elements in curly braces if the assignment is made in the same statement that the array is declared:

```
import java.awt.*;
import java.awt.event.*;

public class ColorEx extends Frame implements ActionListener {
    Color colors[] = {Color.black, Color.blue, Color.cyan,
        Color.darkGray, Color.gray, Color.green,
        Color.lightGray, Color.magenta, Color.orange,
        Color.pink, Color.red, Color.white, Color.yellow};
    int count;
    . . .
```

The constructor sets the size and layout, adding Closer as usual. A button is added along with its listener. The int variable count is used to keep track of the current color. The command setBackground() is used to assign a color to the Frame:

```
    . . .
    public ColorEx() {
        setSize(300,200);
        setLayout(new FlowLayout());
        addWindowListener(new Closer());
        Button b = new Button("Next Color");
        b.addActionListener(this);
        add(b);
        count = 0;
        setBackground(colors[count++]);
        show();
    }
    . . .
```

The actionPerformed() method toggles through the array of colors. The if structure resets the array counter back to zero when it threatens to overshoot the end of the array:[1]

```
    . . .
    public void actionPerformed(ActionEvent e) {
        count++;
        if (count >= colors.length) {
            count = 0;
        }
        setBackground(colors[count]);
    }
    public static void main(String argv[]) {
        new ColorEx();
    }
}
```

The same kind of code will work with GUI components, as is exemplified below. This program displays a Button, Choice, and Checkboxes. Pressing the button toggles the color of the button through the list of basic colors.[2] Selecting the appropriate color from the Choice sets the Choice to that color. Finally, the individual Checkboxes are each their own color; selecting one of them sets the background of the Frame to that color. Here is how the components are arranged:

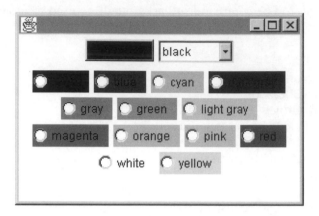

Let's now look at the code, which is interesting because it adds a couple of new features and because it shows how multiple controls need to be treated. The program implements several interfaces to handle all the events generated by the controls. At the class level, there are several interesting features. First, there are three arrays declared, two of which are initialized by listing. The third is an array of Checkboxes. Note that while the Checkbox array is initialized with this statement, each individual Checkbox must still be initialized:

```java
import java.awt.*;
import java.awt.event.*;

public class ColorComps extends Frame
      implements ActionListener, ItemListener {
    Color colors[] = {Color.black, Color.blue, Color.cyan,
          Color.darkGray, Color.gray, Color.green,
          Color.lightGray, Color.magenta, Color.orange,
          Color.pink, Color.red, Color.white, Color.yellow};
    String cnames[] = {"black", "blue", "cyan",
          "dark gray", "gray", "green",
          "light gray", "magenta", "orange",
          "pink", "red", "white", "yellow"};
    int count;
    Button b;
    Choice c;
    CheckboxGroup cbg;
    Checkbox cb[] = new Checkbox[13];
    Panel p1,p2;
    . . .
```

The constructor for the program does the usual things for the Frame. Note that it does not change the default layout. Instead, it uses the default BorderLayout to place two Panels. The first is used for the Button and Choice, while the latter is used for the Checkboxes. Notice too how the for structures are used to handle repetitive initialization steps:

```
. . .
public ColorComps() {
    setSize(300,200);
    addWindowListener(new Closer());
    b = new Button("Next Color");
    b.addActionListener(this);
    p1 = new Panel();
    p1.add(b);
    c = new Choice();
    for (int i = 0; i < cnames.length; i++) {
        c.addItem(cnames[i]);
    }
    c.addItemListener(this);
    p1.add(c);
    add("North",p1);
    count = 0;
    b.setBackground(colors[count++]);
    p2 = new Panel();
    cbg = new CheckboxGroup();
    for (int i = 0; i < cb.length; i++) {
        cb[i] = new Checkbox(cnames[i],cbg,false);
        cb[i].setBackground(colors[i]);
        cb[i].addItemListener(this);
        p2.add(cb[i]);
    }
    add("Center",p2);
    show();
}
. . .
```

Events are handled in two methods. The actionPerformed() method treats the button events, toggling the color of the button through the array of colors. Events from the other two controls are handled by the itemStateChanged() method. That method queries the other two controls for which item is selected, and sets the color accordingly. Note how this is actually much easier for the case of the Choice than for the Checkboxes. In the latter case, we use a for structure to check which Checkbox is selected:

```
. . .
public void actionPerformed(ActionEvent e) {
    count++;
    if (count >= colors.length) {
        count = 0;
    }
    b.setBackground(colors[count]);
```

```
        }
    public void itemStateChanged(ItemEvent e) {
        c.setBackground(colors[c.getSelectedIndex()]);
        Checkbox temp = cbg.getSelectedCheckbox();
        if (temp != null) {
            for (int i = 0; i < cb.length; i++) {
                if (temp.equals(cb[i])) {
                    p1.setBackground(colors[i]);
                    p1.repaint();
                    p2.setBackground(colors[i]);
                    p2.repaint();
                }
            }
        }
    }
    public static void main(String argv[]) {
        new ColorComps();
    }
}
```

9.2   *Text*

We've seen that text can be displayed in a number of the components. Some of these are designed specifically to display text; for example, Label, TextField, and TextArea. The control components display text as an indication of what the control does. Text can also be displayed by a Graphics object in a paint() method. The following program uses this method to write its command-line arguments in a Frame. If we invoke it with the following command line,

```
    java DrawStringEx This is a test
```

we get the following output:

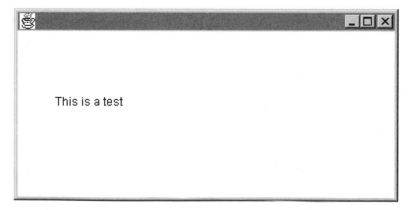

Here's the code:

```
import java.awt.*;

public class DrawStringEx extends Frame {
    String str;
    public DrawStringEx(String s) {
        str = s;
        addWindowListener(new Closer());
        setSize(400,200);
        show();
    }
    public void paint(Graphics g) {
        g.drawString(str,40,100);
    }
    public static void main(String argv[]) {
        String temp = "";
        for (int i = 0; i < argv.length; i++) {
            temp = temp + " " + argv[i];
        }
        new DrawStringEx(temp);
    }
}
```

Displaying text with Graphics is rather different from displaying text with one of the text components. One of the main differences is that text drawn with Graphics is pixel-based, while the text components are not. An important consequence of this is that while pixels can overlap, text components cannot. The following program uses drawString() to display two overlapping strings:

```
import java.awt.*;

public class DrawStringEx2 extends Frame {
    public DrawStringEx2() {
        addWindowListener(new Closer());
        setSize(400,200);
        show();
    }
    public void paint(Graphics g) {
        g.drawString("Here is some text.",40,100);
        g.drawString("A second string.",40,95);
        g.drawString("This is a third string.",58,100);
    }
    public static void main(String argv[]) {
        new DrawStringEx2();
    }
}
```

This is obviously not very useful in and of itself, but this also allows text to overlap with other Graphics objects, drawn with one of the other Graphics commands.

Text can be displayed using different **fonts** as well. Java makes six default fonts available: "Dialog", "DialogInput", "Monospaced", "Serif", "SansSerif", or "Symbol". These are available in any size (in points), and in any of three styles: Font.PLAIN, Font.BOLD, and Font.ITALIC.[3]

While any Java implementation is guaranteed to have all these combinations, the precise font used is not guaranteed. For example, if you specify something to appear as 12-point, Font.PLAIN, "Serif", you can't guarantee precisely which system font with those properties any particular Java implementation will use. Moreover, not all combinations are necessarily distinct.

Using these is straightforward. You simply create a new Font object. Its constructor takes the three arguments above. That Font object can be invoked by the command setFont(), which applies to GUI components and to Graphics. Here is a program showing how these different combinations look when applied to a Label. The program has three Choices, which allow one to select different values for the arguments passed to Font. Every time one of these is changed, setFont() is called to change the Label. Here is how this looks:

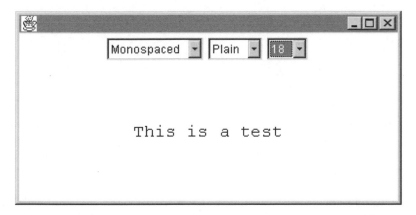

The code makes use of familiar bits. The only new parts are those dealing with Font. Since the program uses Choices, it needs to implement an ItemListener interface. At the class level, a number of variables are initialized, including arrays to hold the font names, styles, and sizes:

```
import java.awt.*;
import java.awt.event.*;

public class FontEx extends Frame implements ItemListener {
    Label l;
    Choice nameC,styleC,sizeC;
    String name;
    int style,size;
    int sizes[] = {9,10,12,18,24,36};
    int styles[] = {Font.PLAIN,Font.BOLD,Font.ITALIC};
    String names[] = {"Dialog","DialogInput","Monospaced",
        "Serif","SansSerif","Symbol"};
    Font font;
    . . .
```

Although large, the constructor is straightforward. Two Panels are used to place the controls and the Label. The controls take a fair amount of space to initialize, but nothing that we haven't seen already:

```
    . . .
public FontEx() {
    setSize(400,200);
    addWindowListener(new Closer());
    Panel p1 = new Panel();
    nameC = new Choice();
    for (int i = 0; i < names.length; i++) {
        nameC.addItem(names[i]);
    }
```

```
        p1.add(nameC);
        nameC.addItemListener(this);
        styleC = new Choice();
        styleC.addItem("Plain");
        styleC.addItem("Bold");
        styleC.addItem("Italic");
        p1.add(styleC);
        styleC.addItemListener(this);
        sizeC = new Choice();
        for (int i = 0; i < sizes.length; i++) {
            sizeC.addItem(Integer.toString(sizes[i]));
        }
        p1.add(sizeC);
        add("North",p1);
        sizeC.addItemListener(this);
        l = new Label("This is a test");
        l.setAlignment(Label.CENTER);
        add("Center",l);
        show();
    }
    . . .
```

The itemStateChanged() method is straightforward as well. Whenever any of the Choices change state, all of them are queried for which item is selected. These indices are used to set the appropriate values in the arrays defined at the outset, and those arrays are used as arguments to the Font constructor. We use the setFont() command to assign this font to the Label:

```
    . . .
    public void itemStateChanged(ItemEvent e) {
        int nameInd = nameC.getSelectedIndex();
        int styleInd = styleC.getSelectedIndex();
        int sizeInd = sizeC.getSelectedIndex();
        font = new Font(names[nameInd],styles[styleInd],sizes[sizeInd]);
        l.setFont(font);
        l.repaint();
    }
    public static void main(String argv[]) {
        new FontEx();
    }
}
```

If we rewrite FontEx using Graphics to draw the string, the result is superficially similar. Here's the code for this change. Notice how the Label has been replaced by the addition of a paint() method. This, in turn, is called by the repaint() command in the itemStateChanged() method:

```java
import java.awt.*;
import java.awt.event.*;

public class FontEx2 extends Frame implements ItemListener {
    Choice nameC,styleC,sizeC;
    String name;
    int style,size;
    int sizes[] = {9,10,12,18,24,36};
    int styles[] = {Font.PLAIN,Font.BOLD,Font.ITALIC};
    String names[] = {"Dialog","DialogInput","Monospaced",
        "Serif","SansSerif","Symbol"};
    Font font;
    public FontEx2() {
        setSize(400,200);
        addWindowListener(new Closer());
        setLayout(new FlowLayout());
        nameC = new Choice();
        for (int i = 0; i < names.length; i++) {
            nameC.addItem(names[i]);
        }
        add(nameC);
        nameC.addItemListener(this);
        styleC = new Choice();
        styleC.addItem("Plain");
        styleC.addItem("Bold");
        styleC.addItem("Italic");
        add(styleC);
        styleC.addItemListener(this);
        sizeC = new Choice();
        for (int i = 0; i < sizes.length; i++) {
            sizeC.addItem(Integer.toString(sizes[i]));
        }
        add(sizeC);
        sizeC.addItemListener(this);
        show();
    }
    public void paint(Graphics g) {
        g.setFont(font);
        g.drawString("This is a test",50,100);
    }
    public void itemStateChanged(ItemEvent e) {
        int nameInd = nameC.getSelectedIndex();
        int styleInd = styleC.getSelectedIndex();
        int sizeInd = sizeC.getSelectedIndex();
        font = new Font(names[nameInd],styles[styleInd],sizes[sizeInd]);
        repaint();
    }
```

```
        public static void main(String argv[]) {
            new FontEx2();
        }
    }
```

However, the display is not quite the same. More of the combinations of styles and font names are distinct. This is because text components are not capable of displaying all combinations of font attributes. Thus a second reason why one might want to use Graphics to display text – rather than GUI components – is because Graphics allows one to make finer choices in combining font names and styles.

Notice another apparent difference between the two displays. By using setAlignment() and the FlowLayout, we were able to center the text when it appears in a text component. The text displayed with Graphics was rooted to a particular pixel location. In fact, this difference is only apparent. Using the FontMetrics class, we can control the position of text precisely. The following program gives an example, showing how FontMetrics allows a text message to stay centered even when the window is resized. Here's a picture of what it looks like (after the window has been stretched some):

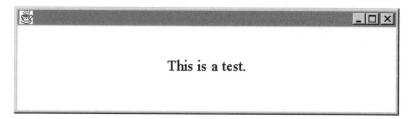

The program contains a few new methods and objects. The first one is that the program implements a ComponentListener interface. This is to respond to the resizing of the window, something that the Java technology does normally with respect to GUI components, but that we have to explicitly invoke with respect to Graphics. The interface requires four methods, only one of which we need to worry about: componentResized(). This method is overridden to include an explicit call to repaint().

The program's constructor is minimal:

```
import java.awt.*;
import java.awt.event.*;

public class FMEx extends Frame implements ComponentListener {
    public FMEx() {
        addWindowListener(new Closer());
        setSize(300,300);
        show();
    }
    . . .
```

The guts of the program are in its paint() method. First, we get the current size of the Frame. This is returned as a Dimension object from the getSize() method. The width and height of the container are stored in two int variables of the Dimension. To locate the center of the container, we divide these by two and store them in new variables.

The method next sets the font that the string will be drawn with, and then collects the FontMetrics class from the current Graphics context. We can use the FontMetrics object to retrieve information about the size of the font and of strings we display with the font. Specifically, we use stringWidth() to get the width of the string when displayed with the current font and getHeight() to get the maximum height of the current font.

When a string is printed with drawString(), its position is fixed with respect to its lower left corner. In other words, the coordinates given to drawString() match the lower left corner of the displayed string. We use the width of the string and the height of the font – along with the previously calculated center of the Frame – to position the string appropriately:

```
. . .
public void paint(Graphics g) {
    String s = "This is a test.";
    Dimension d = getSize();
    int x = d.width / 2;
    int y = d.height / 2;
    g.setFont(new Font("Serif",Font.PLAIN,18));
    FontMetrics fm = g.getFontMetrics();
    int width = fm.stringWidth(s);
    int height = fm.getHeight();
    int newX = x - (width / 2);
    int newY = y + (height / 2);
    g.drawString(s,newX,newY);
}
. . .
```

The remainder of the program is straightforward, including the four required ComponentListener methods and the main method:

```
. . .
public void componentHidden(ComponentEvent e) {}
public void componentMoved(ComponentEvent e) {}
public void componentResized(ComponentEvent e) {
    repaint();
}
public void componentShown(ComponentEvent e) {}
public static void main(String argv[]) {
    new FMEx();
}
}
```

The FontMetrics class is extremely useful for dynamically positioning text. One thing to keep in mind, however, is that one does not want to have too much calculation in the paint() method (or any method that paint() depends on). Putting too much in the paint() method can result in long delays when the screen is redrawn, which can be annoying for your users.[4]

9.3   *Revising* Exp

Let's now take some of what we've learned about GUIs and graphics, and use it to revise the Exp program we developed in chapter 6. As you will see yourself, converting a program from a text-based modality to a graphical one is relatively straightforward, but is often best done from scratch. That is, you should not constrain yourself to reusing each little bit of code that you wrote for the text-based version of the program, but instead build the program around the GUI. This results in a somewhat different organization. However, when the job is done, you'll see that many of the same bits are still there, just in different places.

The new YesNoExp program has five principal components. The first is the abstract parent class ExpGUI. This provides the general shape of an experiment, collects information from the experimenter, and provides some useful methods that many experiment types can make use of. Second, there is the YesNoExp class itself, which provides the specifics of running an experiment where only yes–no responses are recorded. Third, there is the Mats class which reads in the items from a data file. The Mats class is a revision of the old Materials class from the text-based Exp program. Fourth, there is an InfoDialog class for collecting the subject code. Finally, we make use of the Randomizer class of chapter 7 without changes.

Let's look first at the ExpGUI class. There are several main bits to this class and I'll go over each of them. The class imports from java.awt for GUI components, from java.util for vectors, and from java.io for IO. The class defines a number of class-level variables for handling the filenames, the materials, and the results. The constructor initializes the vector and then runs two methods – getInfo() and runExp():

```
import java.awt.*;
import java.util.*;
import java.io.*;

public abstract class ExpGUI extends Frame {
    String filename,file,code,outfilename,outfile;
    Mats m;
    public Vector results;
```

```
public ExpGUI() {
    results = new Vector();
    getInfo();
    runExp();
}
```

. . .

The getInfo() method collects the filenames for IO and the subject code. It does this with two FileDialogs and a new subclass of Dialog called InfoDialog. In all cases, the dialogs are embedded in while structures that prevent the user from simply escaping out of the dialogs without entering the required information. In both cases, the FileDialogs are instantiated with three arguments. The first is the parent Frame. The second is a string message. The third is an int constant that indicates whether the dialog is reading or writing to a file:

```
. . .
private void getInfo() {
    while (file == null) {
        FileDialog fd = new FileDialog(this,
            "Choose the materials file", FileDialog.LOAD);
        fd.show();
        file = fd.getFile();
        filename = fd.getDirectory() + file;
    }
    while (outfile == null) {
        FileDialog fd2 = new FileDialog(this,
            "Choose the results file", FileDialog.SAVE);
        fd2.show();
        outfile = fd2.getFile();
        outfilename = fd2.getDirectory() + outfile;
    }
    while ((code == null) || (code.equals(""))) {
        Dialog id = new InfoDialog(this,"Enter the subject number",true);
    }
    m = new Mats(filename);
}
. . .
```

The runExp() method is abstract, and must be overridden to construct an actual experiment. There is also a randomize() method – that makes use of the Randomizer class already written – for randomizing experimental items. The setCode() method provides an accessor method for the code variable that holds the subject code:

```
. . .
public abstract void runExp();
public Vector randomize(Vector v) {
    Randomizer r = new Randomizer(v);
    Vector temp = r.getVec();
    return temp;
}
public void setCode(String s) {
    code = s;
}
. . .
```

Finally, the saveResults() method provides a way to save results into a file. Notice how the file is opened for appending data by invoking FileWriter with a second boolean argument true:

```
. . .
public void saveResults() {
    try {
        FileWriter fw = new FileWriter(outfilename,true);
        BufferedWriter bw = new BufferedWriter(fw);
        PrintWriter pw = new PrintWriter(bw);
        Enumeration e = results.elements();
        String temp;
        while (e.hasMoreElements()) {
            temp = (String) e.nextElement();
            pw.println(temp);
            pw.flush();
        }
        fw.close();
    } catch (Exception e) {
        e.printStackTrace();
    }
}
}
```

The class has no main method. The subclass that extends ExpGUI must provide its own main method.

The next class is Mats, which is used to read the experimental items from a data file. This file is a revision of the old Materials class. The revision is straightforward. The old Materials class was written using an array which had to be initialized with the first argument of the data file. The new class uses a Vector instead. This means that the first item in the data file should no longer be the number of items in the file:

```
import java.io.*;
import java.util.*;

public class Mats {
    private String filename;
    private Vector items;
    public Mats(String f) {
        filename = f;
        items = new Vector();
        doIO();
    }
    public Vector getItems() {
        return items;
    }
    private void doIO() {
        String line;
        try {
            FileReader fr = new FileReader(filename);
            BufferedReader br = new BufferedReader(fr);
            while ((line = br.readLine()) != null) {
                items.addElement(line);
            }
            fr.close();
        } catch (Exception e) {
            e.printStackTrace();
        }
    }
}
```

The actual file we use to test the program is the same as that used to test Exp, minus the first line:

```
John loves Mary.
Mary loves John.
loves Mary John.
John Mary loves.
```

The next class used is the InfoDialog class. It is a subclass of Dialog, and implements an ActionListener interface to handle button events. It defines several class-level GUI components and an ExpGUI variable for the program that calls it. Notice how the first command of the constructor is a call to the constructor of its superclass. The first argument to that call must be a Frame or a subclass of Frame. The second argument is a string which is set as the title of the Dialog window. The third argument is a boolean which – if true – means that the Dialog has control until it is disposed of:

```
import java.awt.*;
import java.awt.event.*;

public class InfoDialog extends Dialog implements ActionListener {
    Button submit;
    Label label;
    TextField code;
    ExpGUI exp;
    public InfoDialog(ExpGUI e, String s, boolean b) {
        super(e,s,b);
        exp = e;
        setLayout(new FlowLayout());
        label = new Label("Subject code:");
        add(label);
        code = new TextField(" ",10);
        add(code);
        submit = new Button("Submit");
        submit.addActionListener(this);
        add(submit);
        pack();
        show();
    }
    public void actionPerformed(ActionEvent e) {
        exp.setCode(code.getText());
        dispose();
    }
}
```

The last class is an important one: YesNoExp. It imports from java.awt for GUI components, from java.awt.event for its ActionListener, and from java.util for the vector. It defines a raft of class-level GUI components, and for the vector for the experimental items:

```
import java.awt.*;
import java.awt.event.*;
import java.util.*;

public class YesNoExp extends ExpGUI implements ActionListener {
    private Button yes,no,thankyou;
    private Label instructions,item;
    private Panel south;
    private Vector items;
    private Enumeration en;
    . . .
```

The bulk of the work done in running the experiment takes place in two methods. The first runExp() handles the remaining initialization for YesNoExp. The actual experiment is handled in the actionPerformed() method necessitated by the ActionListener interface. The program has two different display conditions. During the experiment, it displays a single label in the "North" zone with instructions. In the "Center", the experimental item is presented in another label. Finally, the response buttons are positioned in the "South", using a Panel. Notice too that we set the fonts for the Labels to be especially large so as to make them more visible. The only tricky part is at the very end of the runExp() method. We set the size of the items Label by initializing it with a very long text string. Then, just before invoking show() – but after using pack() – we change the text of the center Label to an actual experimental item:

```
. . .
public void runExp() {
    instructions = new Label("Is this sentence grammatical?");
    instructions.setAlignment(Label.CENTER);
    instructions.setFont(new Font("Serif",Font.PLAIN,18));
    add("North",instructions);
    item = new Label("The example sentence goes here" +
        " and it can be quite long.");
    item.setAlignment(Label.CENTER);
    item.setFont(new Font("Serif",Font.PLAIN,24));
    add("Center",item);
    south = new Panel();
    yes = new Button("Yes");
    yes.setSize(100,100);
    yes.addActionListener(this);
    south.add(yes);
    no = new Button("No");
    no.setSize(100,100);
    no.addActionListener(this);
    south.add(no);
    add("South",south);
    thankyou = new Button("Thank you!");
    thankyou.addActionListener(this);
    pack();
    items = randomize(m.getItems());
    en = items.elements();
    item.setText((String) en.nextElement());
    show();
}
. . .
```

Here's how it looks:

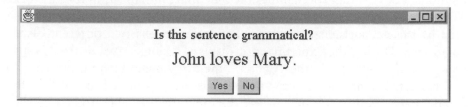

After all the items have been completed, the display changes. The center Label is set to null, The top Label displays a different message, and the response buttons are hidden. In their place, the thankyou button is displayed. It looks like this:

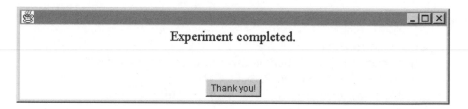

The actionPerformed() method handles the presentation of experimental materials and the change of display. Each time one of the response buttons is pressed, a new string is added to the results vector. These strings indicate the subject, item, and response given. Once there are no more items, the display is changed, and the results are saved by means of a call to saveResults(), an inherited method from ExpGUI. Finally, if a button is pressed and the response buttons aren't visible, then the program must be in its final state and ready to exit.

The method makes use of several new commands for testing the visibility of a component and setting its visibility; for example, isVisible() and setVisible():

```
    . . .
    public void actionPerformed(ActionEvent e) {
      String result;
      if (en.hasMoreElements()) {
        result = code + "\t" + item.getText()
          + "\t" + e.getActionCommand();
        results.addElement(result);
        item.setText((String) en.nextElement());
      } else if (yes.isVisible()) {
        result = code + "\t" + item.getText()
          + "\t" + e.getActionCommand();
        results.addElement(result);
        item.setText(" ");
```

```
            yes.setVisible(false);
            no.setVisible(false);
            instructions.setText("Experiment completed.");
            south.add(thankyou);
            validate();
        } else {
            saveResults();
            System.exit(0);
        }
    }
    . . .
```

Finally, there is a main method that simply instantiates the class:

```
    . . .
    public static void main(String argv[]) {
        new YesNoExp();
    }
}
```

9.4   *Setting up a New Experiment Type*

In this section, I develop another subclass of ExpGUI. The new class is for a psycholinguistic task called **self-paced reading**. The task is useful for assessing the processing time required at different points in a sentence. The subject is presented with a sentence word by word, advancing to each successive word by pressing a key. Reaction times are measured at some particular point in the sentence. After each sentence there is a true–false question, to make sure that the subject is actually paying attention to the sentence and not simply pressing keys aimlessly. Results are then written to a results file:[5]

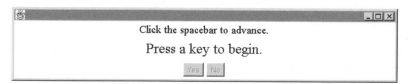

Before looking at the code, let's go through the logic of the program. To create such a program, we must think a bit about what we want it to do. The first thing is to deal with the materials differently, for the materials file has to have a different organization. Each "item" must now comprise several separate bits. First, there must be a string of words, marked so that a reaction time is taken at one point in the string. Second, there must be a question. I add a third field which I call the "code". Instead of writing all the words and the question back to the results file, only the code, the reaction time, and the response to the question are saved. Here's what the materials file looks like for a toy experiment. Lines occur in sequence: the sentence, the question, and the code. The point where the reaction time will be taken is marked with RT:

Java is an interesting RT programming language.
Is java interesting?
1
This is a RT nice program.
Is this a table?
2
That sentence went by too RT quickly.
Did something go by quickly?
3

I set up a special data type – ItemSet – to accommodate this.
After two subjects, the results file looks like this:

```
s1   3   Yes   490
s1   1   Yes   550
s1   2   No    440
s2   2   No    550
s2   3   Yes   440
s2   1   Yes   600
```

Another thing that we'll need is to allow for keyboard input. The subject advances through the sentence by pressing any key of the keyboard. These, as you might expect, generate KeyEvents which are handled by a KeyListener.

Let's now turn to the specific classes of the program. First, let's look at the ItemSet class. It's very straightforward. It simply defines a class that has three string variables. The variables are declared as private, but there are accessors for each of them:

```
public class ItemSet {
    private String sentence;
    private String question;
    private String code;
    public void putS(String s) {
        sentence = s;
    }
    public void putQ(String q) {
        question = q;
    }
    public void putC(String c) {
```

```
      code = c;
   }
   public String getS() {
      return sentence;
   }
   public String getQ() {
      return question;
   }
   public String getC() {
      return code;
   }
}
```

Items are read into a vector by the Mats class as usual, and then converted into a vector of ItemSets. Then they're randomized. However, as currently written, the Randomizer class operates only on a vector of strings. It's rewritten below so as to apply to a vector of any sort of objects. It does this by making use of the Object class, the superclass of all classes in the Java language. If you follow the inheritance trail for any object in Java code, it will eventually reach Object.[6] Notice that we no longer need to cast the result of nextElement(); it automatically returns an Object unless its result is cast as something else:

```
import java.util.*;

public class Randomizer {
   Vector input, output;
   public Randomizer(Vector v) {
      input = v;
      output = new Vector();
      randomize();
   }
   private void randomize() {
      Random r = new Random();
      Enumeration e = input.elements();
      Object let;
      int max,current;
      while (e.hasMoreElements()) {
         let = e.nextElement();
         max = output.size();
         current = r.nextInt(max + 1);
         output.insertElementAt(let,current);
      }
   }
   public Vector getVec() {
```

```
        return output;
    }
}
```

Let's now look at the main class SelfPacedExp. As expected, it extends the ExpGUI class. It imports for GUI, for events, and for the vectors it uses. It implements two interfaces: an ActionListener for button events, and a KeyListener for keystroke events. A number of class-level variables are declared, most of which are GUI components. There is one new feature here: the keyword final as applied to a variable. This means that the variable is a constant, that its value won't be changing over the course of the program. It is customary – though not required – to capitalize the names of constants:

```
import java.awt.*;
import java.awt.event.*;
import java.util.*;
```

```
public class SelfPacedExp extends ExpGUI
        implements ActionListener, KeyListener {
    private Button yes,no,thankyou;
    private Label instructions,item;
    private Panel south;
    private Vector items;
    private Enumeration en;
    private ItemSet currentItemSet;
    private String currentS, currentQ, currentC;
    private StringTokenizer currentTokenizer;
    private boolean begunFlag;
    private final String INSTRUC1 = "Click the spacebar to advance.";
    private final String INSTRUC2 = "Answer the question.";
    private final String INSTRUC3 = "Thank you!";
    private long thisTime,lastTime,timeDiff,theRT;

    . . .
```

The runExp() method of the superclass ExpGUI is overridden as required and most of the GUI initialization takes place here. The arrangement of buttons and labels is essentially the same as in YesNoExp. There are some differences, however. First, items read in by Mats are passed to a method sortItems() before they are randomized. Also, the yes and no buttons are placed, but disabled, with a call to setEnabled().

The KeyListener interface is invoked with a call to addKeyListener(). This means that key events will be registered by the interface's methods when the program – or relevant component – has **focus**. When applied to individual GUI components, focus appears as highlighting. For example, when a FileDialog appears, focus can be shifted by pressing the tab key:

```
   . . .
   public void runExp() {
      begunFlag = false;
      instructions = new Label(INSTRUC1);
      instructions.setAlignment(Label.CENTER);
      instructions.setFont(new Font("Serif",Font.PLAIN,18));
      add("North",instructions);
      item = new Label("This can be a very long question " +
         "so there needs to be lots of room.");
      item.setAlignment(Label.CENTER);
      item.setFont(new Font("Serif",Font.PLAIN,24));
      add("Center",item);
      south = new Panel();
      yes = new Button("Yes");
      yes.setSize(100,100);
      yes.addActionListener(this);
      south.add(yes);
      no = new Button("No");
      no.setSIze(100,100);
      no.addActionListener(this);
      south.add(no);
      add("South",south);
      thankyou = new Button("Thank you!");
      thankyou.addActionListener(this);
      pack();
      items = randomize(sortItems(m.getItems()));
      en = items.elements();
      item.setText("Press a key to begin.");
      yes.setEnabled(false);
      no.setEnabled(false);
      requestFocus();
      addKeyListener(this);
      show();
   }
   . . .
```

The sortItems() method distributes the members of the vector returned by Mats into a vector of ItemSets:

```
   . . .
   private Vector sortItems(Vector v) {
      Enumeration e = v.elements();
      ItemSet is;
      Vector outVec = new Vector();
      while (e.hasMoreElements()) {
         is = new ItemSet();
```

```
            is.putS((String) e.nextElement());
            is.putQ((String) e.nextElement());
            is.putC((String) e.nextElement());
            outVec.addElement(is);
        }
        return outVec;
    }
    . . .
```

Once all the initialization has taken place, the program displays a message that the subject should tap a key to begin the experiment. For the first phase of each experimental item, KeyEvents control the flow of the experiment, displaying new words from the sentence on the screen. The words are obtained from the sentence field of the ItemSet with a StringTokenizer. The program advances word by word with calls to hasMoreTokens().

The key events are handled with the keyTyped() method, one required by the KeyListener interface. The listener also requires two other methods: keyPressed() and keyReleased(). There is a lot in the keyTyped() method, so let's pick it apart slowly. If a key is pressed, the user can be in one of several conditions: (i) it's the beginning of the experiment; (ii) it's the middle of a sentence and there are more words in the sentence; or (iii) it's the end of a sentence and the question now needs to be displayed. This three-way choice is handled with an if structure (marked with comments in the code below). The program defines a boolean flag begunFlag, which is used to keep track of whether the experiment has begun yet. This flag controls whether the keyTyped() method drops into its first condition. The second and third conditions are controlled by whether there are more words in the sentence, whether or not hasMoreTokens() is true.

Finally, the second condition has a subcase. If a key is pressed and it is in the middle of an experimental item *and the current item is the* RT *code*, then two things must happen. First, the RT code itself is not displayed and the next word in the sentence is displayed. Second, the reaction time is recorded in the variable theRT:

```
    . . .
    public void keyTyped(KeyEvent e) {
        //if beginning of exp, advance to first sentence
        if (!begunFlag) {
            currentItemSet = (ItemSet) en.nextElement();
            currentS = currentItemSet.getS();
            currentQ = currentItemSet.getQ();
            currentC = currentItemSet.getC();
            currentTokenizer = new StringTokenizer(currentS);
            item.setText(currentTokenizer.nextToken());
```

```
        lastTime = System.currentTimeMillis();
        begunFlag = true;
    //if middle of sentence
    } else if (currentTokenizer.hasMoreTokens()) {
        String temp = currentTokenizer.nextToken();
        thisTime = System.currentTimeMillis();
        timeDiff = thisTime - lastTime;
        //if middle of sentence and current word is RT, record this RT
        if (temp.equals("RT")) {
            temp = currentTokenizer.nextToken();
            theRT = timeDiff;
        }
        item.setText(temp);
        lastTime = thisTime;
    //if end of sentence, advance to question/buttons
    } else {
        thisTime = System.currentTimeMillis();
        timeDiff = thisTime - lastTime;
        yes.setEnabled(true);
        no.setEnabled(true);
        item.setText(currentQ);
        instructions.setText(INSTRUC2);
    }
}
public void keyPressed(KeyEvent e) {}
public void keyReleased(KeyEvent e) {}
. . .
```

The SelfPacedExp also implements an ActionListener interface to handle button events with the actionPerformed() method. There are three principal parts to it: (i) if a button is pressed after a question and there are more items; (ii) if a button is pressed after a question and there are no more items; and (iii) if the thankyou button is pressed at the end of the experiment.

If a button is pressed after a question and there are more items, then the current results are appended to the results vector, and the next ItemSet is spun off the randomized materials set. If there are no more items, then the old buttons are hidden and the thankyou button is displayed. Finally, if the thankyou button is pressed, then the results are saved and the program is exited:

```
    . . .
public void actionPerformed(ActionEvent e) {
    String result;
    //if question, and there are more, advance to next sentence
    if (yes.isEnabled() && en.hasMoreElements()) {
        requestFocus();
```

```
            yes.setEnabled(false);
            no.setEnabled(false);
            result = code + "\t" + currentC + "\t" +
                e.getActionCommand() + "\t" + theRT;
            results.addElement(result);
            currentItemSet = (ItemSet) en.nextElement();
            currentS = currentItemSet.getS();
            currentQ = currentItemSet.getQ();
            currentC = currentItemSet.getC();
            currentTokenizer = new StringTokenizer(currentS);
            item.setText(currentTokenizer.nextToken());
            thisTime = System.currentTimeMillis();
        //if question, and there are not more, advance to thankyou
        } else if (yes.isEnabled()) {
            requestFocus();
            yes.setVisible(false);
            no.setVisible(false);
            yes.setEnabled(false);
            no.setEnabled(false);
            result = code + "\t" + currentC + "\t" +
                e.getActionCommand() + "\t" + theRT;
            results.addElement(result);
            south.add(thankyou);
            item.setText("");
            instructions.setText(INSTRUC3);
            validate();
        //if thankyou, quit
        } else {
            saveResults();
            System.exit(0);
        }
    }
    public static void main(String argv[]) {
        new SelfPacedExp();
    }
}
```

9.5   *Summary*

This chapter has introduced the basic methods of the Graphics class. When invoked by the paint() method of a container, these allow us to draw shapes, color, and even text. We've spent extra time on the methods associated with text; for example, the Font and FontMetrics classes. Finally, we revised the Exp program so that it now has a GUI. In addition, we wrote a new subclass, demonstrating how to make use of Graphics to collect language data.

9.6   *Exercises*

1. Write a program that uses a Choice control to change the font that this very same control is displayed with.
2. Do the same for Checkbox.
3. Revise the FileDiaEx program so that the font that the file is displayed in is selectable by the user.
4. Write a program that allows you to move a text message around the screen. You should set up control components that let you place the message in at least six locations.
5. The above program can be written using Graphics or a Label for the moving message. Whichever you used above, rewrite it now using the other.
6. Extend the ExpGUI class for another experiment typ.

Notes

[1] No picture of the output is given here, since the images in this book are black and white.

[2] This functionality is missing on Macs. The background color of Button and Choice cannot be changed.

[3] In fact, the Java language makes available any fonts on the system it is running on, but using any of these other fonts disrupts the Java language's platform independence; your program will have problems if you try to run it on a system without the nonstandard font.

[4] There are two usual workarounds for this. One is to avoid using Graphics for displaying text, relying instead on the GUI text components. The other is to make use of independent program **threads**, running in the background, to speed up display calculations. The latter are not treated in this book.

[5] This program uses the keyboard to keep track of reaction times, which is not the most precise input device possible. If you really want very precise reaction times, you should probably make use of a dedicated button box. In addition, precise reaction times depend on many things, such as how many times a second your computer screen is refreshed, when the Java program does automatic **garbage collection**, and what other **threads** are running. Java technology can collect relatively precise reaction time information, but showing how to do this is way beyond the scope of this book.

[6] This is true even for objects that don't overtly extend any other objects. The Object class is the default parent for any object.

Chapter 10
Applets

One of the most exciting Java™ capabilities is its association with the web. Most modern web browsers (**Netscape, Internet Explorer,** and **HotJava**) are written so that Java programs – **applets** – on the web can be downloaded and run directly in the browser. This offers all sorts of opportunities for collecting and analyzing language materials anywhere, on any computer.

While applets are a powerful programming opportunity, using them effectively presents some additional challenges. First, in addition to the new classes and methods required to program applets, there are some additional programming skills required outside of Java technology. Second, there are limits on what can be done with applets, limits that are much more restrictive than standalone programs.

In this chapter, I introduce applets and the ancillary skills needed to program applets effectively.

10.1   *Jar and the JDK*

So far, we have made use of only two of the programs from the Java Development Kit: javac and java. The JDK includes several more and all of the basic ones are listed below. The first four are the really important ones – I include the others only for completeness.

appletviewer   Run applets without a web browser.
jar   Manage *Java ar*chive (jar) files.
java   The launcher for Java applications.
javac   The compiler for the Java code.
javadoc   This generates API-type documentation.

jdb The Java debugger.

javah The C header and stub generator. Used to write native methods.

javap The class file disassembler.

extcheck A utility for detecting jar conflicts.[1]

javakey Key management and digital signatures.[2]

We've already used java and javac quite a bit and I won't say any more about them. Applets are normally run in a web browser; the appletviewer program allows you to test them without a browser. I will deal with the jar tool in depth in this section, but let me say just a little about the other tools here.

The javadoc tool operates on raw Java code that has been commented in javadoc-style to generate API-style documentation. If you haven't already checked out the API, this style of documentation lists all the public methods and variables of a class or set of classes and links items together. The javadoc-style comments in the raw code provide the explanations for each variable or method. This is an extremely useful tool if you're planning on a large suite of classes, especially if you intend for them to be useful to other programmers.

The jdb tool allows you to debug Java programs. It allows you to step through a program incrementally and examine current system properties. Once you know more about programming, it can be quite useful. At the beginning stages, however, it's a little too overpowering to be of much use.

The javah tool is for using Java technology with the C programming language.

The javap tool can be quite useful, even at this stage. If you give it a classname as an argument, it will return all the public methods and variables associated with that class, along with their argument types. For example, if you give it the classname SelfPacedExp (from the previous chapter), you'll get the following:

```
Compiled from SelfPacedExp.java
public class SelfPacedExp extends ExpGUI implements
java.awt.event.ActionListener, java.awt.event.KeyListener {
public SelfPacedExp();
public void actionPerformed(java.awt.event.ActionEvent);
public void keyPressed(java.awt.event.KeyEvent);
public void keyReleased(java.awt.event.KeyEvent);
public void keyTyped(java.awt.event.KeyEvent);
public static void main(java.lang.String[]);
public void runExp();}
```

The extcheck program checks on conflicts between separate jar files that have been installed as **extensions**. Extensions are really an advanced feature and so we will not spend any more time with this.

Finally, the javakey tool for digitally signing jar files has been discontinued.

Returning to the focus of this section, let's look at the jar command. It is a superficially simple tool. What it allows you to do is to compress a set of files into a single file, called a **jar file**. The compression is actually zip compression, but in addition a **manifest** file is created. Programs compressed into a jar file can be run directly without explicitly decompressing them.

The jar tool provides for several nice things. First, it allows you to group together the class files associated with a single program into a single file. Second, it compresses that file. Third, and most important for applets, putting the files associated with your applet in a single jar file means that your user's web browser only has to retrieve a single file, rather than a set of files. This can dramatically affect the speed with which your applet runs.[3]

Running the jar command is straightforward, but there are several little nuances. Imagine that we want to create a jar file for the files associated with the SelfPacedExp program. If all of those files are in a single directory, we switch to that directory, and execute this command:

```
jar cf myjarfile.jar *.*
```

This creates a new file myjarfile.jar in the same directory that contains compressed versions of all the files in that directory. To list the contents of the jar file, the following command is executed:

```
jar tf myjarfile.jar
```

To extract the files from the jar file, first, move the jar file to a new location so that the extracted files do not conflict with their originals. Then type the following:

```
jar xf myjarfile.jar
```

This should recreate all the same files that were originally compressed into the jar file. In addition, it extracts a new directory called Meta-inf, which contains the single file Manifest.mf. The latter is a text file which contains the following virtually useless information:[4]

```
Manifest-Version: 1.0
Created-By: 1.2.2 (Sun Microsystems Inc.)
```

The jar command is invoked with various flags, some of which we have already used. The full list is given below:

c   Creates a new jar file.

t   Lists the contents of a jar file.

x   Extracts files.

f   Allows you to specify the name of the jar file.

v   Generates verbose output.

m   Includes manifest information from a specified manifest file.

0   Add files without compression.

M   Do not create a manifest file.

u   Update an existing jar file.

-C   Changes directories.

Notice that most of these options are *not* indicated with a hyphen.[5] Notice too that if there are filename arguments, then they must occur in the same order as the flags that refer to them. So, for example, if jar is given the flags fm, then the jar filename must occur *before* the name of the manifest file.

Running a program that is in a jar file can occur in three ways. The first is to extract the files as above, and then run java on the extracted class files.

The second method is to include the jar file in your classpath and then invoke the program as usual. For example, if the program is called myprog and all its class files have been put in myjar.jar, the program can be run by typing java -classpath myjar.jar myprog.

The other method (as of Java 1.2) is to run java directly on the jar file. For this to be successful, the manifest file must specify what the **Main-Class** of the jar file is, the name of the class that you would otherwise invoke java with.

To do this, you must edit the manifest file directly. Continuing with the first example above, first extract the manifest from the archive with this command:[6]

```
jar xf META-INF\MANIFEST.MF
```

This will extract the manifest file already described above. Edit it to include the main-class specification, as follows:

```
Manifest-Version: 1.0
Created-By: 1.2.2 (Sun Microsystems Inc.)
Main-Class: SelfPacedExp
```

The first two or more lines may look different. All that you should do is *add* a line like the third. The revised manifest must be added to the jar file, replacing the original manifest, with the following command:

```
jar ufm myjarfile.jar manifest.mf
```

This updates the existing jar file with the manifest file named. To run the program now, use the following command:

```
java -jar myjarfile.jar
```

It is a bit of a hassle to have to modify the jar file by hand in this fashion, but the tradeoff is that all the relevant files are put together. Note that in the example at hand the materials file and the results file *cannot* be read from within the jar file.[7]

10.2   HTML

Another preliminary to programming applets is some knowledge of **HTML**, or hypertext markup language. This is the language used to create basic web pages. A full treatment of HTML is not the focus of this book, but I'll describe enough here so that you can write web pages that can host applets.

The HTML language is composed of **tags**, which are always enclosed in angled brackets. These tags typically mark simple logical formatting; for example, headings, general type faces, paragraphs and the like. Typically, there is a beginning tag and an ending tag, with the ending tag including a leading slash. For example, the highest level of headings would be marked like this:

```
<h1>a heading</h1>
```

The basic skeleton of a web page has two parts: a head and a body. For our purposes, the head can really only contain the title for the web page, with everything else occurring in the body of the page. This gives us the following basic skeleton for a simple web page:

```
<html>
<head>
<title>The title goes here.</title>
</head>
<body>
The body of the page goes here.
</body>
</html>
```

The whole thing is bracketed by <html> tags, as are the head and body sections. The title then goes in the <title> tags.

For example, if we wanted to put the first four sentences of this section on a web page, the raw HTML would look like this:

```
<html>
<head>
<title>Sample paragraphs</title>
</head>
<body>
<h1>HTML</h1>

Another preliminary to programming applets is some knowledge
of <strong>HTML</strong>, or hypertext markup language.
This is the language used to create basic web pages. A full
treatment of HTML is not the focus of this book, but I'll
describe enough here so that you can write web pages that can
host applets.<p>

The HTML language is composed of <strong>tags</strong>,
which are always enclosed in angled brackets. These tags
typically mark simple logical formatting; for example, headings, general
type faces, paragraphs and the like. Typically, there is a beginning tag
and an ending tag, with the ending tag including a leading slash.<p>

</body>
</html>
```

The spacing here – other than word breaks – is completely ignored. I include paragraph breaks here only for convenience, as they help the programmer envision what the page will ultimately display like. Notice also the <strong> tags. Precisely how these are displayed is controlled by the browser. The user can actually specify how they want such tags to be realized. In the early days, all HTML tags were of this "logical" type. As time has passed though, more and more specific tags – for example, for bold face, italics, and so on – have been introduced. Finally, notice the <p> tag for marking paragraph breaks. It is one of the very few tags that are unpaired.[8]

There are several more tags that are of general use. One is the hyperlink tag, that enables the user to click on a word or phrase and be taken to a different web page. For example, imagine you want your user to be taken to the Banana Information Center if he or she clicks on the word "banana" in some sentence. If the address – or **URL** – of the Banana Information Center is www.bananas.org, then you would mark the link as follows:

```
. . . and <a href="http://www.bananas.org">bananas</a> are . . .
```

The tag is symmetric and must be terminated with the </a> tag. The quotes are required and are a common source of error.

A hyperlink tag can also be used to initiate an email message. This enables the user to click on a word or phrase and be automatically sent to their email software, to send an email to the address specified in the link. For example, if you wanted to specify an email address where questions could be emailed about the Banana Information Center, you could do it as follows:

```
. . . and <a href="mailto:myfriend@bananas.org">bananas</a> are . . .
```

Again, the quotes are required and the tag is symmetric.

The essential tag for using applets is the applet tag. It allows you to place an applet at some point in a web page, much as you might place a graphic. The tag is a little more complex than the other tags we have looked at so far. It has a number of parts, some of which are obligatory and some of which are optional. Here is an example of a hypothetical applet tag with only the obligatory bits:

```
<applet code="MyApplet.class" width=200 height=300>
</applet>
```

If you had an applet called MyApplet, this tag would place it at the corresponding point in the web page and reserve the space indicated.

There are many possible options, and in this section I only discuss two. All the applet tag options are exemplified when we start actually writing applets. The first option makes sense of why the tag is symmetric. You can place additional material in between the tags. If the user's web browser isn't configured to run applets, then this other material will be displayed.

```
<applet code="MyApplet.class" width=200 height=300>
You're missing my <strong>very</strong> interesting applet!
</applet>
```

If the applet isn't displayed, then the applet tag is completely disregarded; the amount of space used to display the alternate text is the amount normally required to do so, not the amount originally reserved for the applet.

Another extremely important option for the applet tag is the archive option. If you've put your applet classes into a jar file, you would use this tag to give the name of that file. For example:

```
<applet code="MyApplet.class" archive="myjarfile.jar"
width=200 height=300>
You're missing my <strong>very</strong> interesting applet!
</applet>
```

Again, I'll give examples of this below when we actually write some applets.

10.3   The "Sandbox"

Applets are extremely powerful. They can be delivered over the web and they run on the user's computer, regardless of the kind of computer that is. What this means, though, is that if applets could do all the normal things that programs could do, surfing the web would be a very dangerous proposition. What if a malicious person were to mount an applet on their website that, when downloaded to the user's machine, deleted all the user's personal files? What if the malicious applet sent out spurious email? Without limits, applets might seem like a very bad idea.

For these reasons, applets are sharply restricted in terms of what they can do. The idea is to disallow any function that might damage the user's machine or files. In this section, I go through these limits.

First, while Java programs can normally interact with programs written in other programming languages, this is not possible for applets.

Second, applets cannot read or write to files on the user's machine.

Third, applets cannot make any sort of network connection except back to the host machine that the applet was downloaded from. For example, if you write an applet and put it on your website at the Banana Information Center in Tucson, Arizona, then the applet will not be able to connect a user to the Orange Information Center, although it would be able to connect back to your website in Tucson.

Fourth, while regular Java programs can start other programs on your computer, applets cannot.

Fifth, normal Java programs can query for various system properties that include the user's name, and various file information. Applets cannot do this.

Finally, windows that an applet brings up look different than windows that an application brings up. Depending on the browser, they typically have some sort of warning to the effect that the window is an applet window.

These limits insure that web surfing with your browser configured to display applets is not dangerous.

On the other hand, these limits are serious restrictions on what you can do with an applet. The most constraining are the ones on reading and writing files.[9]

10.4   The Basics of Applets

An applet can be treated rather like a Frame. The biggest difference is that an applet doesn't have a constructor *per se*, but instead uses an init() method. Here is a very simple applet that simply displays a text message:

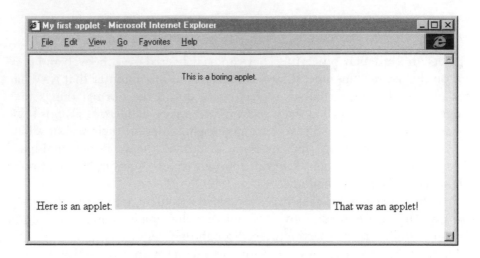

Here is the HTML code that the applet is embedded in:

```
<html>
<head>
<title>My first applet</title>
</head>
<body>
Here is an applet:
<applet code="SimpleApp1.class" width=300 height=200>
Your browser isn't configured for applets!
</applet>
That was an applet!
</body>
</html>
```

The web page is in a file called simpleapp1.html. Finally, here is the code for the applet:

```
import java.applet.*;
import java.awt.*;

public class SimpleApp1 extends Applet {
    Label l;
    public void init() {
        setBackground(Color.yellow);
        l = new Label("This is a boring applet.");
        add(l);
    }
}
```

To display this applet, compile the code with javac as usual, and then open the hosting web page in your web browser.

Let's go through the applet code. The program extends the Applet class, which is in the java.applet package, and that package must therefore be imported. In addition, this particular applet uses graphics objects, and so the java.awt package is also imported. The code is otherwise straightforward, except that the kind of initialization that we would normally see in the class constructor is in the init() method. Notice two differences, however. First, there is no pack() or setSize() command. The size of the applet is set by the HTML size specifications in the applet tag. Second, notice that there is no explicit show() command. The applet is automatically shown when the web page is displayed.

Let's now look at the HTML code and the display. I added text around the applet to demonstrate how the applet object is treated like any other HTML object. If there is no explicit code to force a break between the applet and the surrounding text, then there will be no break. We can easily add reasonable breaks. First, we can add <p> to each side of the applet. We can also center the applet on the page using the (symmetric) <center> tag.

Finally, we can change the size of the applet by changing the height and width specifications in the applet tag. Here is the revised HTML and how the new display looks:

```
<html> <head>
<title>My first applet</title>
</head>
<body>
Here is an applet:
<p>
<center>
<applet code="SimpleApp1.class" width=300 height=50>
Your browser isn't configured for applets!
</applet>
</center>
<p>
That was an applet!
</body>
</html>
```

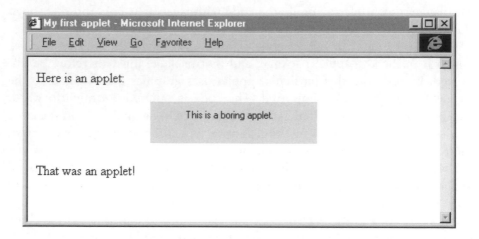

Notice two things. First, making these changes does *not* require that we recompile the SimpleApp1 program with javac. To see these changes, we need only reload the web page in our browser. Second, notice that we now have several examples of nested tags. For example, the paired applet tags are now surrounded by paired tags for centering. Paired tags *cannot* cross. That is, you *cannot* have cases like this:

```
<center><applet . . . >. . . </center></applet>
```

So far, I have assumed that you are viewing your applet with your web browser. If you are making changes in the HTML code of the container page, this is quite convenient, since changes in the HTML can be displayed simply by reloading the page.

On the other hand, if you want to make changes in the Java code of the applet, recompile, and then see the difference, most web browsers will *not* be able to display the difference unless you quit entirely from the browser and restart it. The most convenient way to see changes in the Java code is to use the JDK tool appletviewer.

The appletviewer program would be invoked as follows to display the applet we have been working on:

```
appletviewer simpleapp1.html
```

With the changes that we have made, this would bring up the following window:

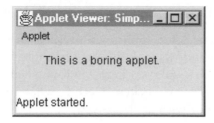

There are several things to notice about this. First, notice that the appletviewer command takes the HTML file's name as an argument. Second, notice that even though appletviewer starts from the web page, it only displays the applet; it doesn't display any of the HTML. The reason for this is that appletviewer uses the size parameters from the HTML file to determine the size of the applet window it displays.

Before going on to more substantive programs, let's see how the archive flag of the applet tag works. First, put the SimpleApp1 program into a jar file with the following command:

```
jar cf myappjar.jar SimpleApp1.class
```

Next, revise the simpleapp1.html file so that the beginning applet tag looks like this:

```
<applet code="SimpleApp1.class"
archive="myappjar.jar" width=300 height=200>
```

Finally, copy the new jar file and the HTML file to a new directory (or delete the old SimpleApp1.class file) so you can be sure you're running the program from the jar file, and not the original class file. To view the new configuration, restart your web browser or use appletviewer.

10.5   Fancier Stuff

Let's do a little bit more with applets. I won't dwell on those aspects of applets that are the same as standalone programs, but focus instead on those aspects that are different.

In general, applets are the same as regular programs. Except for the security restrictions above and the lack of an overt constructor, applet classes can do the same things as other Java classes. For example, applets can have any number of methods and can call any number of other classes. The principal domains in which applets are different are: (i) windows and dialogs; (ii) IO; and (iii) images and sounds.

10.5.1   Windows and dialogs

There are three differences for applets with respect to windows and dialogs. The first thing is that windows look different in applets. The following applet contains a button which displays a new window when clicked. The window closes when the close box is clicked. Here is what the window looks like when the program is run with appletviewer:

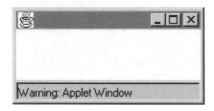

The HTML is pro forma:

```
<html>
<head>
<title>An applet window</title>
</head>
<body>
<applet code="AppWin.class" height=100 width=100>
</applet>
</body>
</html>
```

The main applet class is also straightforward. It must import from java.applet for the applet, from java.awt for the button, and from java.awt.event for the ActionListener. The program creates a button that displays an instance of MyWindow when clicked:

```
import java.applet.*;
import java.awt.*;
import java.awt.event.*;

public class AppWin extends Applet implements ActionListener {
    Button b;
    MyWindow mw;
    public void init() {
        b = new Button("Show window.");
        b.addActionListener(this);
        add(b);
        mw = new MyWindow();
```

```
    }
    public void actionPerformed(ActionEvent e) {
        mw.show();
    }
}
```

The MyWindow class is a simple one. It merely creates a window and adds a WindowListener to handle when the window is closed. Here is the code for MyWindow. The only thing to note is that the WinDis class takes MyWindow as an argument. We will see why this is necessary shortly:

```
import java.awt.*;

public class MyWindow extends Frame {
    public MyWindow() {
        setSize(200,100);
        addWindowListener(new WinDis(this));
    }
}
```

Finally, here is the WinDis class, a subclass of WindowAdapter. When the close box is clicked, we want the window to disappear, but the applet should keep running. The appropriate command is dispose(), but this command applies to the Frame, not the WindowAdapter. That is why the constructor for WinDis takes MyWindow as an argument. Since MyWindow is a subclass of Frame, it inherits all its methods, including dispose():

```
import java.awt.event.*;

public class WinDis extends WindowAdapter {
    MyWindow parent;
    public WinDis(MyWindow p) {
        parent = p;
    }
    public void windowClosing(WindowEvent e) {
        parent.dispose();
    }
}
```

A second difference between applets and standalone programs is that applets cannot call dialogs directly. Recall that dialogs take their parent Frame as an argument. The problem is that applets themselves aren't really Frames. Hence, there is nothing to pass as an argument to the constructor for Dialog (or, for that matter, FileDialog).

There is, however, a workaround for this that is quite straightforward. Since applets can create Frames, they can then use those Frames in turn to call a dialog. It is a simple matter to extend the AppWin applet to show how this works (which I leave as an exercise).

Finally, the third difference is that applets cannot bring up FileDialogs at all. Recall that the security limits on applets prevent them from reading and writing files. Hence, they can't use FileDialogs.

10.5.2   IO: parameters and URLs

Applets can accept and display information through the relevant GUI components, but not through file IO or, obviously, command-line input. They can, however, accept input in two other ways: applet parameters and URLs.

Applet parameters are entered in the host HTML page as follows:

```
<html>
<head>
<title>Applet parameter test</title>
</head>
<body>
<applet code="AppParam.class" width=200 height=100>
<param name=thetext value="This worked just fine.">
Your browser can't run applets!
</applet>
</body>
</html>
```

The parameter goes in its own tag with two attributes, one indicating the parameter name, and the other indicating the value. Note that the case of the name is irrelevant and that quotes are required for the value only when it includes spaces or special characters.

The Java code to respond to parameters is straightforward:

```
import java.applet.*;
import java.awt.*;

public class AppParam extends Applet {
    Label l;
    public void init() {
        String text = getParameter("THETEXT");
        l = new Label(text);
        add(l);
    }
}
```

The value of the parameter is returned with the command getParameter() applied to the name of the parameter.

At this point, the only obvious value of applet parameters is that they allow you to make changes to an applet in the HTML code, rather than the Java code, sparing you the need to recompile your applet. Another advantage of applet parameters is that they allow you to write a more general purpose applet that can be tailored to different HTML contexts easily.

Another way applets can read in information is through URLs. That is, an applet can make a connection over the web to a remote host. Note, however, that the security restrictions on an applet prevent connecting to any host other than the one the applet came from. This means that the applet can read from other files/URLs on the same host.

Here's an example that shows how this works. This applet displays the text of a file given as an applet parameter. Just for fun, I set the value of the parameter to be the HTML page itself. Here's what the display looks like:

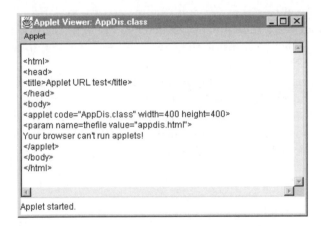

The HTML code is straightforward and – since the applet parameter was set to name the exact same HTML file – it is displayed in the screenshot above.

The Java code includes a few new features and is given below. The program imports from java.applet because it's an applet, from java.awt because it uses the GUI, from java.io because it uses readers, and from a new package java.net because it uses URLs. It then defines several class-level variables. The init() method is simple. It changes the layout so that the size of the TextArea is automatically set. It gets the filename to be read from the applet parameter, and then it sets the text of the TextArea with a defined method getText():

```
import java.applet.*;
import java.awt.*;
import java.io.*;
import java.net.*;
```

```
public class AppDis extends Applet {
   TextArea ta;
   String filename;
   public void init() {
      setLayout(new BorderLayout());
      ta = new TextArea("");
      add("Center",ta);
      filename = getParameter("THEFILE");
      String theText = getText();
      ta.setText(theText);
   }
   . . .
```

The getText() method includes some new bits. First, it makes use of a new object URL, which it creates with two arguments. The first is the URL returned by the applet method getCodeBase(). This returns the host of the applet, and guarantees that we don't get a security violation.[10] The filename variable was set from the applet parameter in the init() method above. Notice that the URL is declared inside the try/catch loop. This is, in fact, necessary, as creating a URL can throw an exception.

The URL is read with an InputStreamReader. The reader takes a Stream as an argument and the URL provides this with the URL method openStream(). The rest of the method is analogous to IO techniques that we've already seen many times. Note that we handle errors a little differently here; the error message is displayed in the TextArea:[11]

```
   . . .
   private String getText() {
      String temp = " ";
      String line;
      try {
         URL url = new URL(getCodeBase(),filename);
         InputStreamReader isr = new InputStreamReader(url.openStream());
         BufferedReader br = new BufferedReader(isr);
         while ((line = br.readLine()) != null) {
            temp = temp + "\n" + line;
         }
         br.close();
      } catch (Exception e) {
         temp = "Couldn't open URL!";
      }
      return temp;
   }
}
```

You should enter different files as the parameter for AppDis to see that other files can be displayed as well.

Opening a URL connection is an important technique for a surprising reason: it is the *only* way for an applet to save information. There are a number of ways to use this technique, and I discuss several in appendix C, but the basic idea is that whatever information you wish to save from running the applet can be sent back to the host as a request to open a new connection. For example, imagine you have an applet that collects a user's favorite color and name. The applet then tries to open a new page from the host that includes the color and name as part of the request.

There are various ways to have the web server running on the host machine save and even process that information. This involves some quite advanced techniques and so is deferred to the appendix.

10.5.3 Images and sounds

It is quite easy to play sounds and display images with applets. Both can be done with standalone programs as well but, for some reason, the Java language was designed so that it would be very straightforward to do both in applets.

Sounds in 8-bit .au format can be played in applets with the AudioClip object. First, the sound is retrieved with getAudioClip(), and then played with play(). The following applet shows how this is done. The display includes a single button that plays a sound.[12] Here's the HTML:

```
<html>
<head>
<title>Applet Sound Test</title>
</head>
<body>
<applet code="AppSound.class" width=100 height=50>
<param name=thefile value="chirp1.au">
Your browser can't run applets!
</applet>
</body>
</html>
```

The Java code is as expected. Notice that the AudioClip is created with two arguments, the first of which is returned by the getCodeBase() method:

```
import java.applet.*;
import java.awt.*;
import java.awt.event.*;
```

```
public class AppSound extends Applet implements ActionListener {
    Button b;
    AudioClip ac;
    public void init() {
        b = new Button("Play");
        String s = getParameter("THEFILE");
        ac = getAudioClip(getCodeBase(),s);
        b.addActionListener(this);
        add(b);
    }
    public void actionPerformed(ActionEvent e) {
        ac.play();
    }
}
```

You can play sounds in a standalone Java program as well, but it's a little tricky.[13] The following program creates a display similar to the preceding applet, but in a standalone Frame. The code is simple. Other than the usual commands to create a window, button, and appropriate listeners, the program must obtain the AudioClip with the command Applet.newSoundClip(). This is a static method of the Applet class, which means that we must import from java.applet, even though the program is standalone. In addition, even though the action all takes place on a single computer, the command takes a URL as an argument (which means that we must import from java.net as well. The whole program is given here:

```
import java.awt.*;
import java.awt.event.*;
import java.applet.*;
import java.net.*;

public class SoundProg extends Frame implements ActionListener {
    Button b;
    AudioClip ac;
    public SoundProg() {
        setSize(100,90);
        setLayout(new FlowLayout());
        addWindowListener(new Closer());
        b = new Button("Play");
        b.addActionListener(this);
        add(b);
        getTheClip();
        show();
    }
    private void getTheClip() {
```

```
        try {
           URL url = new URL("file:chirp1.au");
           ac = Applet.newAudioClip(url);
        } catch (Exception e) {
           e.printStackTrace();
           System.exit(0);
        }
     }
     public void actionPerformed(ActionEvent e) {
        ac.play();
     }
     public static void main(String argv[]) {
        new SoundProg();
     }
  }
```

Images can be handled in a much more symmetric fashion. Here's an example of an applet that displays a centered image:[14]

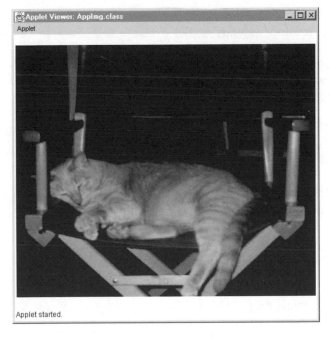

For completeness, here is the HTML:

```
<html>
<head>
<title>Applet image test</title>
</head>
<body>
```

```
<applet code="AppImg.class" width=500 height=450>
Your browser can't run applets!
</applet>
</body>
</html>
```

The Java code follows. The program uses the getSize() method to determine the size of the applet. The image is retrieved with getImage(), taking a URL as an argument again. As usual, the prefix of the URL is obtained with getCodeBase() to prevent a security violation. The paint() method does the work of calculating where to draw the image and then drawing it. Image size is obtained with getWidth() and getHeight(). These commands take the applet (or Frame) itself as an argument. The command to draw the image is drawImage(). Notice that it too takes the applet (or Frame) as an argument:

```
import java.applet.*;
import java.awt.*;
import java.net.*;

public class AppImg extends Applet {
   Image i;
   int bigX,bigY,littleX,littleY;
   public void init() {
      Dimension d1 = getSize();
      bigX = d1.width;
      bigY = d1.height;
      try {
         URL url = new URL(getCodeBase(),"puck.jpg");
         i = getImage(url);
      } catch (Exception e) {
         e.printStackTrace();
      }
   }
   public void paint(Graphics g) {
      littleX = i.getWidth(this);
      littleY = i.getHeight(this);
      int x = (bigX / 2) - (littleX / 2);
      int y = (bigY / 2) - (littleY / 2);
      g.drawImage(i,x,y,this);
   }
}
```

Drawing images in a standalone application is only slightly more difficult. The following program displays a centered image just like the applet above. The only substantive difference is the command used to retrieve the image:

Toolkit.getDefaultToolkit().getImage()

The Toolkit is a class for retrieving properties from the local graphics system. To obtain an actual instance of this class, one uses the static command getDefaultToolkit(). The getImage() command is a method of the Toolkit obtained. Note that, unlike the getImage() method of Applet, this method takes a URL or filename as an argument:

```
import java.awt.*;

public class ImgProg extends Frame {
    Image i;
    int bigX,bigY;
    public ImgProg() {
        bigX = 550;
        bigY = 550;
        setSize(bigX,bigY);
        addWindowListener(new Closer());
        i = Toolkit.getDefaultToolkit().getImage("puck.jpg");
        show();
    }
    public void paint(Graphics g) {
        int littleX = i.getWidth(this);
        int littleY = i.getHeight(this);
        int x = (bigX / 2) - (littleX / 2);
        int y = (bigY / 2) - (littleY / 2);
        g.drawImage(i,x,y,this);
    }
    public static void main(String argv[]) {
        new ImgProg();
    }
}
```

10.6   *Summary*

This chapter has introduced applets and some of the related machinery required to make applets work; that is, HTML and the JDK jar command. We have focused on those aspects of applets that differ from standalone programs, largely dealing with those areas where the security restrictions on applets dictate a different approach.

While applets are an exciting area for Java technology, keep in mind that the security restrictions on IO mean that collecting data via an applet necessitates some sophistication. Some techniques for this are discussed in appendix C.

10.7   Exercises

1. Extend the AppWin applet so that it can bring up a dialog window.
2. Write an applet that displays an image and plays a sound when the user clicks on the image with the mouse.
3. Extend the ExpGUI program with an experimental technique of your choice that uses sound.
4. Rewrite the PigLatin program as an applet.

Notes

[1] Since Java 1.2.

[2] Discontinued after Java 1.1.

[3] Applets do not *need* to be put in a jar file, but they often are.

[4] This is for a jar file created with Java 1.2. Other versions of the Java language put slightly different information in this file.

[5] This format and most of the specific flags are the same as the Unix command tar.

[6] This is the appropriate command when running jar under Windows. For Unix, reverse the slash. For Mac, this is not an option, as Java 1.2 is not yet available.

[7] The jar command works as described here for both Unix and Windows. For the Mac, it is a little different. First, there is a GUI for jar that allows the user to set many (but not all) of the command-line options. In addition, there are some added restrictions on jar for Mac. First, files to be added to a jar file must be in the same directory as the jar program itself. Second, the jar program on a Mac doesn't work with directories of files, but only with bare files.

[8] There is now a </p> tag, but it is not strictly required.

[9] There are some workarounds. We'll see in this chapter that it is possible to read files from the host the applet was loaded from. In appendix C, I discuss ways in which information can be saved.

[10] If you entered that information directly, that would work on some web browsers, but not on others.

[11] Applets can print to standard output, but when the applet is run in a browser, the user would have to call up that display in the browser's "java console" (or equivalent).

[12] The sound is of a bird chirping. The file is among those available on the website.

[13] This is only possible as of Java 1.2. Many more sound types can be played in 1.2 as well; for example, aiff, wav, midi, and rmf.

[14] In this case, the image is of our family cat Puck. The file is among those available on the website.

Appendix A
Java™ 1.0, 1.1, 1.2, 1.3, and Swing

Throughout this book, I have tried to use Java version 1.1 as consistently as possible. Occasionally, I have used features from Java 1.2, pointing out when and why that was done. In this chapter, I review the main versions of the Java language and the principal differences that separate them. There are three main releases of the Java technology: 1.0, 1.1, and 1.2.[1] There were numerous minor releases as well, but the main differences among versions occurred at these three points. In the following, I will outline how the first and third versions differ from the second (which we've been using so far).

A.1 Java 1.0

The main difference between Java 1.1 and the older Java 1.0 is in the event model. The newer Java 1.1 event model involves listeners, which are separate classes added to individual components.

The initial event model was rather different. It was based on **handler** methods. There is really no longer any reason to write Java programs that use this model, but you still find many examples of it in older code, so it's useful to know something about it. It's still possible to write code using the older model, but the javac compiler will issue a **deprecation** warning if you do.

Classes such as Applet, Frame, and Dialog all inherit from a class called Component. The Component class defines a set of methods for handling events:

```
action()
mouseEnter()
mouseExit()
mouseMove()
```

```
mouseDown()
mouseDrag()
mouseUp()
keyDown()
keyUp()
gotFocus()
lostFocus()
handleEvent()
```

Most of the methods are obvious in what they handle. The action() method treats what an ActionListener handles in the newer model; the handleEvent() method treats most anything left over, not handled by one of the other specific methods. One thing to keep in mind is that all of these methods return a boolean, rather than being void, as in 1.1.

To handle an event in 1.0 style, you simply add (override) the relevant method to your container. Recall the ButtonEx4 program on page 109. The following program shows how it would be redone using the older event model. First, there is no importing from java.awt.event as no listeners are invoked. In fact, that subpackage didn't even exist in the 1.0 event model. Second, no listeners are added in the class's constructor method.

Next, the program has two handler methods. The first is action() for the button event. If the event is handled, the method returns true; if not, the method returns false. To determine if the relevant event is a button event (and not some other sort of event), the target of the event is evaluated. The target variable of Event holds the component that was the target of whatever event took place:

```
import java.awt.*;

public class ButtonEx4OLD extends Frame {
    Button b;
    int i;
    public ButtonEx4OLD() {
        i = 1;
        setSize(300,300);
        setLayout(new FlowLayout());
        b = new Button("Press me!");
        add(b);
        show();
    }
    public boolean action(Event e, Object arg) {
        if (e.target.equals(b)) {
            System.out.println("Button press #" + i++);
            return true;
        }
```

```
      return false;
   }
   . . .
```

The other event handler is the lower-level handleEvent() method to close the window. First, we need to check that the low-level event that actually took place was a window-closing event. We check the id variable to see if it matches the constant defined for window-closing. If it matches, we take the appropriate action. In any case, the method allows the event-handling methods of the superclasses of the current class to have their shots at the current event by passing the event on up the hierarchy with the command super.handleEvent(e):

```
   . . .
   public boolean handleEvent(Event e) {
      if (e.id == Event.WINDOW_DESTROY) {
         System.exit(0);
      }
      return super.handleEvent(e);
   }
   public static void main(String argv[]) {
      new ButtonEx4OLD();
   }
}
```

The older event model was clearly simpler in some respects. There were no listeners and the event-handling methods were always available. On the other hand, *all* of the events of any particular Frame or Applet had to be passed through the same methods, which meant that there could be some pretty extensive code to determine what components were associated with what events.

A.2   Java 1.2

Java 1.2 (or Java 2) includes a number of new features, some of which we've already seen. For example, we saw that the StringBuffer and Random classes include new methods in Java 1.2. In addition, many more sound types can be played in the newer version of the Java language. The biggest changes, however, involved data types and GUI.

A.2.1   Collections

Java 1.2 reorganized the Vector and Hashtable classes into the new **collections** framework, adding a number of very useful new classes. The collections framework introduces a lot of functionality, and to explain all of it would take us far beyond the scope of this book. In this section, I'll only introduce two of the more useful classes in the framework – TreeSet and TreeMap – and show how to use them.

TreeMap

We've already seen one of the new classes: TreeMap, in the TMTest program on page 97. This allows for a hash where the hashkeys are returned in sorted order. The keys are stepped through using the iterator() method, which returns an instance of Iterator.

TreeSet

The TreeSet class is quite straightforward. Elements returned by an Iterator over this class are sorted. Thus adding and then retrieving elements from a TreeSet results in a very efficient sorting of those elements. Here's a simple example showing how the command-line arguments can be sorted:

```
import java.util.*;

public class TSTest {
    public static void main(String argv[]) {
        TreeSet ts = new TreeSet();
        for (int i = 0; i < argv.length; i++) {
            ts.add(argv[i]);
        }
        Iterator i = ts.iterator();
        String temp;
        while (i.hasNext()) {
            temp = (String) i.next();
            System.out.println(temp);
        }
    }
}
```

A.2.2   Swing

In the first two releases of the Java technology, GUI components made use of the local operating system. For example, drawing a window on a Mac meant making use of the MacOS to help draw the window. Likewise, drawing a window in the Windows operating system took advantage of that operating system's window-drawing capabilities.

While this helped to speed things up, and it guaranteed that Java programs took on a look and feel appropriate to the local system, it put the Java language somewhat at the mercy of the different operating systems it was operating on. To rectify this, and to guarantee that Java GUI components would perform exactly the same on any computer, Swing – a rich set of GUI components, that are independent of the local operating system – was released.

In this section, I'll go through some of the basics of converting a typical GUI program to a Swing-based program. I'll also show some of the advantages of doing so. However, the Swing GUI components are very powerful, and a full description would warrant a book in its own right.

Most of the GUI components that I've discussed in this book have a Swing equivalent. All of these components are part of the new javax.swing package, rather than java.awt:

Applet	JApplet
Frame	JFrame
Dialog	JDialog
FileDialog	JFileChooser + JDialog
Panel	JPanel
Button	JButton
Checkbox	JCheckbox, JRadioButton
Choice	JComboBox
Menu	JMenu
MenuBar	JMenuBar
MenuItem	JMenuItem
Label	JLabel
TextArea	JTextArea
TextField	JTextField

Most of these can be used in virtually the same way as their java.awt equivalents. There are two key differences. First, laying components out in a container now has an intermediate level: the ContentPane. You must first retrieve the ContentPane for the container with getContentPane(), and then the usual commands work; for example, add(), setLayout(), and so on.

The second difference is that you no longer override paint() to do graphics. Instead, you override the paintComponent() method of some component to do graphics. The awkward part about this is that you no longer apply graphics directly to a container, but to a component. Thus to do graphics in a JFrame, JApplet, or JDialog, you must add a JPanel and override its paintComponent() method.

Let's look at some examples. First, the following program is a simple conversion of the ButtonEx4 program on page 109. First, the program imports from java.awt for the FlowLayout, from java.awt.event for the listener, and javax.swing for the GUI components. The code is the same except that the add() and setLayout() commands operate on the ContentPane returned by getContentPane():

```
import java.awt.*;
import java.awt.event.*;
import javax.swing.*;

public class SwingButton extends JFrame implements ActionListener {
    JButton b;
    int i;
    public SwingButton() {
        i = 1;
        addWindowListener(new Closer());
        setSize(300,300);
        getContentPane().setLayout(new FlowLayout());
        b = new JButton("Press me!");
        b.addActionListener(this);
        getContentPane().add(b);
        show();
    }
    public void actionPerformed(ActionEvent e) {
        System.out.println("Button press #" + i++);
    }
    public static void main(String argv[]) {
        new SwingButton();
    }
}
```

The addition of a ContentPane means that container-level graphics must be discarded. Instead, graphics must be specific to some GUI component. The following program shows how we can revise the GrEx1 program on page 127 to handle the graphics in a JPanel.

The main class of the program is SwingGraph, which is a subclass of JFrame. It differs from GrEx1 in that there is no paint() method, and a newly defined class MyJPanel is added to the ContentPane:

```
import javax.swing.*;

public class SwingGraph extends JFrame {
    public SwingGraph() {
        setSize(200,300);
        addWindowListener(new Closer());
        getContentPane().add(new MyJPanel());
        show();
    }
    public static void main(String argv[]) {
        new SwingGraph();
    }
}
```

The MyJPanel class is a subclass of JPanel which includes only the method paintComponent(). All the graphics commands that had been in the paint() method of GrEx1 are in this method:

```
import javax.swing.*;
import java.awt.*;

public class MyJPanel extends JPanel {
    public void paintComponent(Graphics g) {
        g.drawLine(15,50,100,50);
        g.drawOval(15,100,30,30);
        g.fillRect(15,150,100,80);
    }
}
```

One very nice consequence of the Swing components is that you can set your program to exhibit a different look and feel, regardless of the operating system you are operating in. In other words, you can make your program look like a Unix (or Motif) program, even if it's running under Windows (or vice versa). Here is an example of a program that can display three JRadioButtons and a JButton in any of three modes. The "Metal" look and feel is the cross-platform Java language look and feel:[2]

The program imports from javax.swing for the Swing components, then from java.awt.event for the listener, and from java.awt for the FlowLayout. The JRadioButtons are put together in a ButtonGroup, so that selecting one deselects the others. As with any Swing application, the GUI components are added to the ContentPane, rather than directly to the JFrame:

```
import javax.swing.*;
import java.awt.event.*;
import java.awt.*;

public class LookChooser extends JFrame implements ActionListener {
    ButtonGroup bg;
    JRadioButton metal,windows,motif;
    JButton quit;
    public LookChooser() {
        quit = new JButton("Quit");
        quit.addActionListener(this);
        addWindowListener(new Closer());
        getContentPane().setLayout(new FlowLayout());
        metal = new JRadioButton("Metal");
        metal.addActionListener(this);
        metal.setSelected(true);
        windows = new JRadioButton("Windows");
        windows.addActionListener(this);
    motif = new JRadioButton("Motif");
    motif.addActionListener(this);
    bg = new ButtonGroup();
    bg.add(metal);
    bg.add(windows);
    bg.add(motif);
    getContentPane().add(metal);
    getContentPane().add(windows);
    getContentPane().add(motif);
    getContentPane().add(quit);
    . . .
```

The last step of the constructor sets the look and feel to "Metal" with the command UIManager.setLookAndFeel(). Notice that this has to take place in a try/catch structure, since it can throw an exception:

```
  . . .
  try {
     UIManager.setLookAndFeel("javax.swing.plaf.metal.MetalLookAndFeel");
  } catch (Exception e) {
     e.printStackTrace();
  }
  pack();
  show();
  }
  . . .
```

The actionPerformed() method sets the look and feel, based on which JRadioButton is selected. Since the components are already displayed, there is a special command to update them – SwingUtilities.updateComponentTreeUI():

```
    . . .
    public void actionPerformed(ActionEvent e) {
        String name = e.getActionCommand();
        String look = "";
        if (name.equals("Metal")) {
            look = "javax.swing.plaf.metal.MetalLookAndFeel";
        } else if (name.equals("Windows")) {
            look = "com.sun.java.swing.plaf.windows.WindowsLookAndFeel";
        } else if (name.equals("Motif")) {
            look = "com.sun.java.swing.plaf.motif.MotifLookAndFeel";
        } else if (name.equals("Quit")) {
            System.exit(0);
        }
        try {
            UIManager.setLookAndFeel(look);
        } catch (Exception ex) {
            ex.printStackTrace();
        }
        SwingUtilities.updateComponentTreeUI(this);
        pack();
    }
    public static void main(String argv[]) {
        new LookChooser();
    }
}
```

Notes

[1] Java 1.2 and the subsequent 1.3 are also referred to as Java 2.
[2] The literature describes a fourth Mac look and feel, but that is only supposed to be available on the Mac. Java 1.2 is not available for Macs before Mac OS 10.

Appendix B
Pattern Matching

Regular expressions allow one to fine-tune a search. In this section, I describe two optional components that add this power to the Java™ langauge. One package is called OROMatcher and the other is gnu.regexp.

B.1   Regular Expressions

Regular languages are defined in formal language theory as those closed under three operations: **union, concatenation**, and **Kleene star**. Assuming a basic vocabulary a,b,c, then [ab] represents the union of a and b; that is, a or b. The expression ab represents the concatenation or sequence a followed by b. Finally, $a*$ represents zero or more instances of a. Combining these allows us a convenient way to define a possibly infinite set of strings. For example, the expression $a[bcd]e$ stands for the following three strings: *abe*, *ace*, and *ade*.

B.2   Perl Syntax

Both of the packages described in this section use the same representation of extended regular expressions as the programming language Perl. There are whole books on regular expressions, so in this section, I review some of the simpler aspects. The basic symbols are given in the following list (adapted from the ORO documentation):

| Alternatives separated by |; for example, (a | b).
{n,m}   Match at least n but not more than m times.

{n,}   Match at least n times.
{n}   Match exactly n times.
*   Match 0 or more times.
+   Match 1 or more times.
?   Match 0 or 1 times.
.   Matches everything except \n.
^   Matches the beginning of a string or line.
$ Matches the end of a string or line.
[abcd]   Character classes; for example, a or b, or c or d.
[a-z]   Ranges; for example, from a to z.
[^a]   Complement; for example, not a.
\b   Matches a word boundary.
\B   Matches any boundary that isn't a word boundary.
\A   Matches only at the beginning of a string.
\Z   Matches only at the end of a string (or before a new line at the end).
\n   New line.
\r   Carriage return.
\t   Tab.
\f   Formfeed.
\d   Digit [0-9].
\D   Nondigit [^0-9].
\w   Word character [0-9a-zA-Z].
\W   A nonword character [^0-9a-zA-Z].
\s   A whitespace character [\t\n\r\f].
\S   A nonwhitespace character [^ \t\n\r\f].
\xnn   A hexadecimal representation of a character.
\cD   Matches the corresponding control character.
\nn or \nnn   A octal representation of a character (unless a backreference).
\1, \2, \3, and so on   Matches whatever the first, second, third, and so on parenthesized group matched (backreference).

Here are a few examples:

$a[^b]c{3,} matches a line-initial sequence composed of a, some character other than b, and at least three instances of c.

\t[a-d]*(ka|st) matches a tab followed by any number of a, b, c, or d followed by the sequence ka or st.

a.(bc)*d+e matches an a followed by some character, followed by **any** number of repetitions of the sequence bc, followed by one or more instances of d, followed by an e.

What we want is to be able to use regular expressions to represent search terms, and this is precisely what these two packages do.

B.3   ORO

A company called **ORO** (for "Original Reusable Objects") developed an excellent package called **OROMatcher** for adding regular expressions to the Java language. It is a wonderful package, and although the ORO company no longer exists, the package is still distributed for free over the Internet by Daniel Savarese, the company founder.[1]

The OROMatcher package is quite complex. I give a single example here of how it can be used. The program listed below provides a simple example of how a file can be searched using OROMatcher.

Use of the package involves downloading and decompressing the files from the website mentioned in footnote 1. The com directory and its contents should be put in the same directory as the class file that you are attempting to compile and run.[2]

The program below takes two arguments at the command line, the first a regular expression and the second a filename. The program then searches through the file for any matches and prints them out.

The code makes liberal use of the ORO package. First, it imports from java.io for IO, and the ORO package for all the regular expression methods. It defines a number of variables. The string variable theTerm holds the first command-line argument, the regular expression. The matcher is obviously what does the matching. The compiler converts the regular expression into something Java can interpret: the Perl5Pattern. The Perl5StreamInput holds the input stream read from the file.

The program then includes a try/catch structure for the IO and compiling of the regular expression. The interesting part of the code is the while structure, which loops over the Perl5InputStream searching for matches, printing them out whenever it finds them:

```
import java.io.*;
import com.oroinc.text.regex.*;

public class OroEx {
   public static void main(String argv[]) {
      String theTerm = argv[0];
      Perl5Matcher matcher = new Perl5Matcher();
      Perl5Compiler compiler = new Perl5Compiler();
      Perl5Pattern thePattern;
      Perl5StreamInput theInput;
      MatchResult result;
      try {
         thePattern = (Perl5Pattern) compiler.compile(theTerm);
         FileReader fr = new FileReader(argv[1]);
```

```
            theInput = new Perl5StreamInput(fr);
            while(matcher.contains(theInput, thePattern)) {
                result = matcher.getMatch();
                System.out.println(result.toString());
            }
        } catch(Exception e) {
            e.printStackTrace();
        }
    }
}
```

The OroEx program allows for very sophisticated searches using all the regular expression symbols listed above.

B.4 gnu.regexp

The gnu.regexp package was originally programmed by Wes Biggs, and is available for free from **Gnu**.[3] This package is rather easy to use, although it does have some quirks. First, download and decompress the files. They include API documentation and a jar file gnu-regexp-X.jar (where X is the version number). To use it, include the jar file in your classpath and invoke the classes with the appropriate import statement. I give a small program below exemplifying how to do this. This program takes a regular expression and a filename as command-line arguments. It then prints out all lines in the file that match the pattern.

The program is called GnuREEx. It imports from java.io for IO and from gnu.regexp for regular expressions. The key bit of code is the class RE provided by gnu.regexp. The constructor for RE takes a regular expression as a string for its argument, compiling it into something that the JVM can interpret. To test for a match, we call the getMatch() method. If this returns null, then there is no match. Here is the code:

```
import gnu.regexp.*;
import java.io.*;

public class GnuREEx {
    public GnuREEx(String pat, String file) {
        String line = " ";
        try {
            RE re = new RE(pat);
            FileReader fr = new FileReader(file);
            BufferedReader br = new BufferedReader(fr);
            while ((line = br.readLine()) != null) {
```

```
            if (re.getMatch(line) != null) {
                System.out.println(line);
            }
        }
        br.close();
    } catch (Exception e) {
        e.printStackTrace();
    }
  }
  public static void main(String argv[]) {
    new GnuREEx(argv[0],argv[1]);
  }
}
```

Notes

[1] The OROMatcher package can be obtained from http://www.savarese.org. It is also available from Gnu (http://www.gnu.org).

[2] Alternatively, you can put the com directory anywhere in your classpath, a variable that you can set on the command line or globally in some systems. As of Java Z, it can also be put in the jre\lib\ext\ directory of your JDK installation.

[3] Gnu stands for "Gnu is not Unix": http://www.gnu.org.

Appendix C
Servlets and CGI

In this appendix, I very briefly discuss server-side Java™ programming. The basic idea is that we want a way for the applets that we write to communicate results that can be saved on the webserver.

While this is an extremely important topic, it is also a terribly complex one. This section simply lays out the basics of how to run Java programs on a server. I introduce three techniques for recovering applet information: server logs, Java CGI programming, and Java servlet programming.

C.1   HTTP Logs and GET

The simplest technique for saving results from an applet is to use the webserver logs on the host machine. Your web pages and applets are displayed by a webserver program. Such programs typically keep a log of all connection requests. If these logs are available to you, then you can use them to keep track of results from your applets.

The basic idea is as follows. You write an applet that collects some sort of information. A user makes a link to the hosting web page, causing your applet to be loaded in the user's web browser. The user interacts with the applet, which collects the relevant information. At the end of the interaction, the applet encodes the information into a request for a subsequent web page from your host. The webserver on your host keeps track of that request in a log file, which you can search through to recover the relevant information.

On my own server – where we are running the **Java WebServer** – the relevant log file is called access_log. It is a series of lines, each of which contains the following bits (along with various codes that I'll leave aside). First, there is an **IP** (internet protocol) number, which designates the machine that is making the request for a web page. Second, there is the date. Finally, there is a specification of the **HTTP** (hypertext transfer protocol) request. Here is a typical line of the log file.

```
123.456.789.000 - - [24/Aug/2000:13:33:09 -0600] "GET
/apage.html?info=x+y HTTP/1.0" - -
```

The 12-digit number at the beginning of the line is where the IP number of the requesting machine goes. The date is given in square brackets in the middle of the line. Finally, the HTTP request is given in quotes.

Let's look a little more closely at the HTTP request. It is composed of three bits. The first is the type of request, here GET. There are several other possibilities – POST, PUT, DELETE, TRACE, and OPTIONS – but the type that we are interested in is indeed GET. The next part of the request field is the precise URL requested. Here, I've given a more complex request type that includes a specific page designation plus a **query string**. The page designation comes first, and then the optional query string goes from the question mark to the end. The last part of the request field is the version of HTTP used.

When requesting a page from a server, it is always possible to include a query string. If a normal static HTML page is requested – and there is no special server filtering going on – then the query string is ignored. On the other hand, if the "page" requested isn't really a page, but a call to a program on the server, then the query string can be quite useful.

The query is the part after the question mark, and has a typical structure. First, it is separated from the URL proper by a question mark. It is generally a series of pairings of variables and values – for example, x=10 – separated by ampersands – for example, x=10&y=3&j=xyz. Letters and numbers appear normally, but anything else is encoded. Space is represented as +, and everything else is represented by a hexidecimal code. (Java provides classes for encoding and decoding strings into this form: URLEncoder.encode() and URLDecoder.decode().) The other thing to keep in mind about the query string is that some webservers impose an upper limit on the length of the URL plus query of approximately 240 characters.

To take advantage of this mechanism to save information, we need two things. First, we need an applet that saves information and returns it to the webserver in a query string. Second, we need a program that can search through the access_log for particular URLs, saving any query strings that are associated with them (along with the date/time, and perhaps the connecting machine).

Here is a simple applet that collects a user's name and age, and then returns that to the server as a query string. The applet is embedded in a simple web page that does nothing else except set a title:

```html
<html>
<head>
<title>Name and Age</title>
</head>
<body>
<applet code="NameAge.class" width=500 height=100>
</applet>
</body>
</html>
```

The applet itself displays two TextFields for entering the name and age information, two Labels so that it's clear what goes in what field, and a button to submit the information. The applet uses a BorderLayout and several Panels to arrange the components suitably. Here is what the applet looks like in the appletviewer:

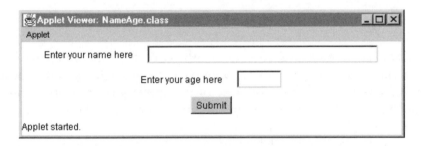

The code for the applet has two principal bits. First, there is the GUI, which is straightforward, although this is the first time that we've used so many Panels:

```java
import java.applet.*;
import java.awt.*;
import java.awt.event.*;
import java.net.*;

public class NameAge extends Applet implements ActionListener {
    private Panel top,center,bottom;
    private Label ageLabel,nameLabel;
    private TextField name,age;
    private Button submit;
    public void init() {
        setBackground(Color.white);
        setLayout(new BorderLayout());
```

```
        top = new Panel();
        center = new Panel();
        bottom = new Panel();
        ageLabel = new Label("Enter your age here");
        nameLabel = new Label("Enter your name here");
        name = new TextField(40);
        age = new TextField(5);
        submit = new Button("Submit");
        top.add(nameLabel);
        top.add(name);
        center.add(ageLabel);
        center.add(age);
        submit.addActionListener(this);
        bottom.add(submit);
        add("North",top);
        add("Center",center);
        add("South",bottom);
    }
    . . .
```

The actionPerformed() method contains the code for submitting the results. It does this by requesting another web page, thankyou.html, and appending the results as a query string. Because of the applet security restrictions, this second page must of course be on the same webserver. This is guaranteed by using the getCodeBase() method.

The results are massaged into the usual query string form. First, each TextField is encoded, and then appended to an appropriate variable name with =. The two statements are separated from each other with &, and separated from the URL proper with ?. The applet then instructs the browser to display a new web page with the command showDocument(). This is a method of the AppletContext class, and the reigning AppletContext is obtained with the method getAppletcontext():

```
    . . .
    public void actionPerformed(ActionEvent e) {
        String results;
        results = "name=" + URLEncoder.encode(name.getText()) + "&" +
            "age=" + URLEncoder.encode(age.getText());
        try {
            URL url = new URL(getCodeBase(),"thankyou.html?" + results);
            getAppletContext().showDocument(url);
        } catch (Exception ex) {ex.printStackTrace();}
    }
}
```

This results in a new line in the log file that might look like this:

```
123.456.789.000 - - [24/Aug/2000:13:33:09 -0600]
"GET /thankyou.html?name=Mickey+Mouse&age=12 HTTP/1.0" - -
```

We then use an appropriate version of our Grep program to periodically search through the access_log file for instances of thankyou.html.

This is a very simple way to deal with the problem of recovering information from an applet, but it suffers from two shortcomings. First, it relies on having access to the log files and on those files being updated in a reasonable fashion. Your server may be configured so that you do not have access to these files. Alternatively, you may have access, but the files may be updated on a schedule that is either mysterious or inconvenient. The second problem is that this method requires that you search through the log files at periodic intervals.[1]

C.2   CGI

The usual treatment of applet information is with a CGI script.[2] This essentially means a computer program that runs on the webserver in response to an HTTP request. The logic is identical to the log file treatment in the previous section up to the point at which the applet issues the showDocument() command.

At that point, we replace the thankyou.html page with the name of a CGI script. When the request reaches the webserver, the server runs the CGI program. That program can do any number of things, including sending HTML code back to the user's web browser and saving information supplied in the request's query string.

Such programs are usually kept in a special directory, typically cgi-bin. CGI scripts are extremely powerful devices and you should check to make sure that they are available to you on your server. Many system administrators disallow users from posting their own CGI scripts because of the damage that they can do.

The only problem for us is that Java is not the most common choice for writing CGI scripts. As a consequence, we have to do a little extra work if we want to write our CGI in the Java language. What we'll do is write a "bridging" script in one of the more common scripting languages to call our Java code.

Two very common choices for CGI scripts are Perl or shell script. I'll give examples of bridging code in each. The following is an example of the kind of code that you need to write to use Perl as a bridging language. Let's assume that your Perl CGI bridge is called jbridge.pl. Your applet would then use a URL such as the following to call it (with a suitable query string):

```
http://www.myhost.org/cgi-bin/jbridge.pl?name=Mickey&age=12
```

The code for the bridge script would look like the following (note that this is written in Perl, of course, and *not* in the Java language):

```
#!/usr/local/bin/perl
exec("/usr/bin/java MyJavaCGI $ENV{QUERY_STRING}");
```

The first line tells the webserver that this is Perl. It does so by telling it the full path of your Perl interpreter. Thus if Perl is somewhere else on your system, then you'd give it a different path. The second line is a Perl command that says to run the Java program on the hypothetical classfile MyJavaCGI. Again, you have to give the full path for your Java interpreter. The query string is transmitted to your Java program via the Perl variable $ENV{QUERY_STRING}.

This method will work on any machine that has Perl installed. However, it may require some tweaking. For example, running the JavaWebServer under Windows 95, I massaged the Perl bridge code as follows:

```
#!perl
exec("javaw MyJavaCGI $ENV{QUERY_STRING}");
```

Since the path is set in the autoexec.bat file to include the location of the Perl and Java programs, the call to those two programs need not include full file locations.[3] In addition, I used the command javaw, which is otherwise like java except that it doesn't bring up a DOS window that has to be closed manually.

Another common scripting choice on Unix machines is shell script. Here is an example of bridging code using this:

```
#!/bin/sh
/usr/bin/java MyJavaCGI "$QUERY_STRING"
```

The first line again tells the webserver that this is shell script. The second line invokes the Java program on the named classfile. Here, the query string is transmitted with the appropriate shell variable.

The Java program then simply takes the query string, extracts the relevant information, and appends it to a suitable file. Shown below is a sample program that does this. Recall that either bridge script calls the Java classfile with an argument representing the query string. Hence the constructor for this class must be passed a string argument. The program first decodes that argument. It then collects the current date and time with the Java program class Date. It then appends everything to a file of results nameage.txt. Since this CGI script is called by the applet's showDocument() command, it returns HTML code which is then displayed in the user's browser:

```java
import java.io.*;
import java.util.*;
import java.net.*;

public class NameAgeCGI {
    public NameAgeCGI(String s) {
        String theInput = "";
        try {
            theInput = URLDecoder.decode(s);
        } catch (Exception e) {
            e.printStackTrace();
        }
        Date today = new Date();
        try {
            FileWriter fw = new FileWriter("nameage.txt",true);
            BufferedWriter bw = new BufferedWriter(fw);
            PrintWriter pw = new PrintWriter(bw);
            pw.println(today.toString() + "\t" + theInput);
            pw.flush();
            pw.close();
        } catch (Exception e) {
            e.printStackTrace();
        }
        System.out.println("Content-type: text/html\n\n");
        System.out.println("<html><head><title>Thank" +
            "you!</title></head>");
        System.out.println("<body>Thank you</body></html>");
    }
    public static void main(String argv[]) {
        new NameAgeCGI(argv[0]);
    }
}
```

Notice, incidentally, that when HTML is generated on the fly like this it must be preceded by a statement about the nature of the content. This enables the receiving browser to interpret the HTML appropriately.

This technique is superior to the preceding one in that the results are saved as they come in. However, this way of doing things relies on an awkward bridging script.

C.3   Servlets

The most elegant way to save information submitted over the web is with a Java **servlet.** Servlets are very much like CGI scripts, except for the following properties. First, servlets are written exclusively in the Java language. Second, servlets require no bridging scripts. Third, servlets are loaded *once* into memory and persist as long as the webserver is running. Fourth, each time a user accesses a servlet, a new **thread,** or program instance, is created. Independent threads allow a servlet to deal with many requests simultaneously.

The downside of servlets is that they require additional Java packages. Fortunately, these are all downloadable for free from Sun.[4] In addition, however, not all web browsers support servlets. Moreover, like CGI scripts, servlets are powerful, and your local system may not allow this power to all users.

Like CGI scripts, servlets typically reside in a special directory, typically called servlets. Moreover, they are invoked with a slightly tricky URL. Imagine that we have written a servlet to save name–age information from the NameAge applet that we have called NameAgeServlet. We would alter the URL that the applet calls as follows:

http://www.myhost.org/servlet/NameAgeServlet?name=Mickey&age=12

Notice that although the servlet would be placed in a directory called servlets, the URL looks as if the servlet is in a directory called servlet.

Let's now look at a servlet that does the work of NameAgeCGI: NameAgeServlet. The program imports from java.io for writing to the file and for generating the HTML. It imports from java.util for the Date class. It imports from two new packages for the servlet-specific classes: javax.servlet and javax.servlet.http. The program itself inherits from HttpServlet. This class includes methods for dealing with any sort of HTTP request. Since the request that we are generating is a GET request, we override the doGet() method of HttpServlet. This method takes an HttpServletRequest and an HttpServletResponse as arguments. In addition, rather than dealing with the various exceptions that this method can throw using try/catch structures, we simply specify that the method throws exceptions of the relevant sort:[5]

```
import java.io.*;
import java.util.*;
import javax.servlet.*;
import javax.servlet.http.*;

public class NameAgeServlet extends HttpServlet {
    public void doGet (HttpServletRequest req, HttpServletResponse res)
        throws ServletException, IOException {
        . . .
```

HttpServletRequest and HttpServletResponse have a number of methods available for determining the nature of the query and specifying the nature of the response. First, we extract the query string from the request with getQueryString(). We retrieve the current date, and then write both to the results file:

```
. . .
String query = req.getQueryString();
Date today = new Date();
FileWriter fw = new FileWriter("nameage.txt",true);
BufferedWriter bw = new BufferedWriter(fw);
PrintWriter pw = new PrintWriter(bw);
pw.println(today.toString() + "\t" + query);
pw.flush();
pw.close();
. . .
```

We next specify that the text sent is to be HTML with the setContentType() command. We obtain the output Writer with getWriter(). We then output the HTML using println():

```
. . .
res.setContentType("text/html");
PrintWriter out = res.getWriter();
out.println("<html><head><title>Thank you</title></head>");
out.println("<body>Thank you!</body></html>");
    }
}
```

If this option is available to you, going with servlets is the best way to go of the three. There are many more things that can be done with them, but that would take us far afield. What I have gone through here is sufficient for you to write programs that collect data with applets and save that data to a central location on your server.

Notes

[1] This, of course, can be automated in different ways. For example, on a Unix machine, you could set your search program up as a cron job run at appropriate intervals.
[2] This acronym is *usually* understood as **Computer Gateway Interface**.
[3] Note that if the machine on which you run this script has multiple users, then you cannot assume that your personal path definition will be available to the webserver.
[4] The appropriate URL is http://www.javasoft.com.

[5] The attentive reader might wonder why we haven't done this before instead of using the more annoying try/catch structure. The use of a throws clause doesn't excuse the programmer from catching the exception; it simply passes the buck up to the next higher level. Here, there is exception-catching code already written into the HttpServlet class to handle these exceptions.

Index